Irish Impressions

To the long-suffering wives of the Directors, without whose support this endeavor would not be possible.

IRISH IMPRESSIONS

by

G.K. Chesterton

Norfolk, VA
2002

Irish Impressions.

Copyright © 2002 IHS Press.

First published in 1919 by W. Collins Sons & Co. of London.

Preface, footnotes, typesetting, layout, and cover design copyright 2002 IHS Press.
All rights reserved.

ISBN: 0-9714894-5-9

    Library of Congress Cataloging-in-Publication Data

Chesterton, G. K. (Gilbert Keith), 1874-1936.
  Irish Impressions / by G.K. Chesterton.
    p. cm.
  Originally published: London : W. Collins, c1919.
  ISBN 0-9714894-5-9
  1. Ireland--Civilization. 2. Irish question. I. Title.

DA962 .C4 2002
941.5082'1--dc21
                                                   2002027371

Printed in the United States of America.

This edition has largely preserved the spelling, punctuation, and formatting of the London 1919 edition.

IHS Press is the only publisher dedicated exclusively to the Social Teachings of the Catholic Church.
For information on current or future titles, contact:

IHS Press
222 W. 21st St., Suite F-122
Norfolk, VA 23517
USA

Table of Contents

	PAGE
Preface	7
The Directors, IHS Press	
Introduction	15
Dr. Dermot Quinn	

CHRONOLOGY OF IRISH HISTORY..........22

IRISH IMPRESSIONS

    I. Two Stones in a Square..........25
    II. The Root of Reality..........31
    III. The Family and the Feud..........43
    IV. The Paradox of Labour..........52
    V. The Englishman in Ireland..........63
    VI. The Mistake of England..........72
    VII. The Mistake of Ireland..........83
    VIII. An Example and a Question..........97
    IX. Belfast and the Religious Problem..........111

SUGGESTIONS FOR FURTHER READING..........148

"...the men of this island had once gone forth, not with the torches of conquerors or destroyers, but as missionaries in the very midnight of the Dark Ages; like a multitude of moving candles, that were the light of the world."

Preface

Gilbert Chesterton visited Ireland in 1918, ostensibly as a recruiting agent for the British Army, but simultaneously as a sincere and devoted friend of Irish freedom. The visit had many repercussions, but the most practical fruit was this book.

To the uninitiated the title *Irish Impressions* might convey the idea of a kind of travelogue written by a journalist with a sharp eye and a nice line in humor; and in one sense it is. But it is a travelogue that deals only *tangentially* with Ireland as a landmass, for this "travelogue" is concerned principally with the Irish soul – with its suffering and pain, its desires and dreams, its violence and its compassion – which has been molded down the centuries by the hammer of oppression acting upon the anvil of Irish Catholicism, itself permeated by a mystical love of the Land of Youth and woven into the very fabric of Gaelic life. The book looks at history as a succession of events molded by Men and Ideas, written in words, in stone, in blood – and framed by the Providence of Almighty God.

When Chesterton landed in Ireland in 1918, he could not have known that the year was going to be so momentous, not only in the struggle of the Irish for their national independence, but also for successive British governments even unto our day; for 1918 was to be the birth of a new phase in Irish and British history, and the death of a previous way of life.

Dorothy Macardle in her authoritative work, *The Irish Republic 1916–1923*, opens her chronological history in these words:

> Although, at the beginning of 1918, the [Irish] Volunteers were re-organized, and although a determination to resist conscription, if necessary, by force of arms existed throughout the country, there was no intention among Republicans to attempt a second insurrection during the year. The Volunteers

and the new Sinn Fein, united under De Valera's leadership, concentrated on strengthening the movement on its political side. It was foreseen that when the European War ended and a Peace Conference came into session, the claims of nations long denied their freedom would be heard. Ireland was to be prepared to send representatives to that Peace Conference – representatives, not of a small party, but of a majority of the nation, who would be in a position to base Ireland's claim on an irrefutable declaration of the will of the people and on the basic principle of government by consent.

The first thing to note is that good numbers of Irish men were armed and ready to fight. They were not on the offensive – as yet – but they were prepared defensively. This is important, for it had not been that way a mere two years earlier. Vincent MacDowell, for example, in his work, *Michael Collins and the Brotherhood* (1997), characterized the changing mood of the Irish people this way: "In the beginning, there had been bewilderment over the suddenness of the [Easter] Rising, disgust and cynicism over the bungling from a military point of view, with divided commands and countermands. This was gradually replaced with sympathy, as day after day the announcements of the executions was given in terse and unfeeling military language." It was a classic, if typical, example of British government lack of comprehension; if you like, an almost innate inability to see that Words and Symbols had meaning in Ireland, as they had in England – but not the same meaning in too many cases.

A reading of the Irish situation in 1918 is not pleasant reading, for it is replete with actions and events that brought little credit upon the British government. Oppression was extensive; the civil and military courts were busy; newspapers were regularly suppressed; letters and telegrams were censored; patriots were harassed and imprisoned; and conscription of the Irish for service at the front in France was in the air. Every day brought grim news and foul deeds – and with every step forward in this process the Constitutional nationalism espoused and epitomized by John Redmond, the leader of the Irish Parliamentary Party, died slowly and surely. Indeed, Redmond's death in 1918 was symbolic of the fate of the whole Constitutional-nationalist position; as Macardle says, "[Redmond] and his followers were duped and betrayed." Whilst Lloyd

George led the Redmondites a merry dance about Irish Home Rule – an offer allegedly intended to satisfy Irish national aspirations – he was writing to Edward Carson in May 1916: "My dear Carson, we must make it clear that at the end of the provisional period [of Home Rule], Ulster does not, whether she wills it or not, merge with the rest of Ireland."

Now into this seething cauldron of violent emotions stepped an individual – not yet visible to the outer world – who was to challenge the British Empire through multi-level action that was to range from the "cultural" – Gaelic sport, the Irish language and literary revival and so on – through to extensive networking, intelligence-gathering, fund-raising and physical force. It was a strategy of co-ordinating the works and wills of the maximum number of Irish men and women in the service of Ireland. It was largely a new strategy, and its implementation was very largely down to one man: Michael Collins.

Those who have seen Neil Jordan's film *Michael Collins* (1996), will be aware of the central importance of Collins in this crucial post-1916 Rising period – though his existence, let alone his centrality, was barely visible in official Irish history books for decades before. One point nevertheless remains that needs to be stressed: that the man, Chesterton, who had come to recruit Irish men to fight on the bloody fields of France, had influenced the man, Collins, the Irish Republican, in the most profound of ways. Collins learned some of his *methodology* from Chesterton, and took much of his political and economic *inspiration* from the Jolly Giant of Beaconsfield. It is a delicious irony and paradox, and one that Chesterton would have enjoyed tremendously.

In his highly readable biography, *Michael Collins: A Life* (1997), James Mackey relates that Collins met Sir William Darling, a British government official, in 1921. He writes:

> They discussed books at great length and discovered a mutual interest in the novels of G.K. Chesterton. It transpired that Michael's favourite was *The Napoleon of Notting Hill*; Darling concluded that the young Irishman was "almost fanatically attached to it," as he recorded in his memoirs, *So It Looks To Me*, published in 1952.

This fact is of more than passing interest, for *The Napoleon of Notting Hill* teaches many a profound lesson. It portrays the struggle of a small nation against the pretensions of Empire; and its relevance is not merely that in Chesterton's book the victory comes to the small nation, but also that the processes of struggle bring about a re-discovery of the true soul of the *imperial* nation. The lesson is that once a nation casts off the artificial burden of Empire, it becomes free to be itself again. Such a lesson could hardly have been lost upon a mind as fine as Collins's.

Chesterton's book also provides the framework of Catholic patriotism. He counterposes the real heroism and sacrifice of patriotism to the smug contentedness and inertia of imperialism; he shows that small nationality not only seeks its rights but also its duties – including the duty which demands that the legitimate rights of other nationalities be respected. Most important of all, Chesterton's book demonstrates that a small nation which is cut off from its spiritual roots risks ruin, in the same way that a man who loses his head risks losing his body, too.

So much for the political inspiration drawn from Chesterton. And the methodology? In Mackey's book, we are told that in 1916, Count Joseph Plunkett – one of the leaders of the 1916 Rebellion – "lent Michael a copy of Chesterton's novel, *The Man Who Was Thursday*, and particularly drew the budding revolutionary's attention to the precept of the President of the Central Council of European Anarchists that 'if you don't seem to be hiding nobody hunted you out.'" Mackey justly comments: "It was a lesson Michael learned well, later raising unobtrusiveness to a high art."

It might be objected, of course, that the case for Chestertonian influence over the young Collins has been exaggerated; yet the facts speak for themselves. At a time when the world was dividing itself between the defenders of Capitalism and the advocates of Socialism, Chesterton and his small band of fellow intellectuals were promoting the virtues of what came to be known as Distributism; a view of the world that supported the small man and the large family; that put the national before the international; and the genuine freedom and happiness of the Common Man before the social control and economic imperatives of Government and Board Room. All things being equal, Michael Collins should have opted for one or other of the supposedly antipathetic creeds of Capitalism and Socialism, given the sheer magnitude of money, power and influence at their disposal. Yet in his work, *The Path to Freedom*, Collins writes:

> The development of industry in the New Ireland should be on lines that exclude monopoly profits. The products of industry would thus be left sufficiently free to supply good wages to those employed in it. The system should be on co-operative lines rather than on the old commercial capitalistic lines of huge joint stock companies. At the same time, I think we shall avoid State Socialism which has nothing to commend it in a country like Ireland, and in any case, is a monopoly of another kind.

It is not the only statement of its kind in Collins's book, and it goes to show that Chesterton had influence in Ireland where he probably would have least expected it.

As we have seen, the year 1918 was crucial in very many ways, not least by the fact that it gave birth to the War of Independence – where Irish Republicans went from the defensive to the offensive as the full weight of the British Empire was brought to bear upon the tiny population of Ireland. Traditionally, it has been argued that the attack at Soloheadbeg, County Tipperary in January 1919 – led by Dan Breen and Sean Tracy – was the opening shot in the War of Independence, but T. Ryle Dwyer has shown in his highly documented work, *Tans, Terror and Troubles: Kerry's Real Fighting Story* (2001), that the Kerry Brigade of the IRA has a better claim to that honor since it had, under the leadership of Tom McEllistrim, attacked the Royal Irish Constabulary barracks at Gortatlea in April 1918. Dates notwithstanding, one thing is clear: the Words, the Symbols and the Actions of the Irish and British parties to the conflict meant wholly different things one to the other. Where the Irish demanded "freedom," the British saw only "sedition and treason"; when the Irish sought refuge and consolation in the Irish language and in the Gaelic heritage, the British saw only "a return to the primitive," something wholly inferior to the "civilization" bestowed by the British Empire; when the Irish Volunteers maintained strict discipline during 1917 and 1918, in spite of tremendous provocation of all kinds, the British saw only "weakness." This inability to find a common language necessarily led to confusion, resentment, misunderstanding and conflict.

Seen in this light, it may be reasonably argued that *Irish Impressions* still teaches many lessons which are as applicable today to the problems of the unresolved conflict in the North of Ireland as they were in Chesterton's day. Though such a proposition may seem incredible, it is not: Truth is not an attribute weighed down by Time. It stands alone, upright and unflinching amidst the thundering storms of history.

Since the end of the Irish Civil War in 1922, the Irish have undergone many changes – most, arguably, for the worst. They are more anglicized than they ever were; they have never been as uprooted from the soil as they are now; and their Catholic faith, which was clasped to their bosoms throughout the centuries of persecution, grows ever weaker as the poisons of indifferentism, secularism, ecumenism and consumerism take their toll. Yet one should take care not to confuse the Clothes for the Man. One is trivial, the other substantial; and a Soul, individual or national, can no more change its nature than can a Pear become a Peach. The Japanese have suffered similarly since 1945, having become "Americanized" – but only the superficial will fail to notice that in Japan the concept of Ritual and the Samurai spirit remain just below the surface.

What, then, of the possibility for Peace in the North of Ireland, over 80 years from the writing of *Irish Impressions*? Chesterton's contribution is to remind us to ignore the appearances and grasp the *realities*. In spite of superficial changes which could fall away in a moment, there remain the Irish and British *Souls*, that must be enabled to speak to one another if there is to be any hope of Peace. And no meaningful conversation can take place unless the Words and Symbols used bear the *same* connotations; and unless it is unflinchingly admitted that there can be no real Peace if it is not founded upon Justice. Carefully worded documents which do not address fundamental issues directly do not constitute Peace, even if there is an absence of violence. As Chesterton states in *Irish Impressions*: "I will say here, once and for all, the hardest thing that an Englishman has to say of his impressions of another great European people; that over all those hills and valleys our word is wind, and our bond is waste paper."

That is still the case today, but the meaning has wider implications now. When Chesterton wrote he was speaking only about the Catholic Irish, though it is becoming evident that it could quite easily be applied more and more to the Protestants of the North. For they see themselves increasingly isolated, misunderstood, "betrayed" by the governments of Westminster. Why has this come about? Perhaps it is because, despite all their protestations, the Protestants of the North have become more Irish than they have realized or even wanted. Living in close proximity with the Irish for centuries, sharing a substantial core of Christian doctrine, adopting indigenous customs and habits, drawn from Gaelic stock and intermarrying on a wide scale, it was inevitable that the Scottish Planter community would approximate more and more to the Irish Soul – and in so doing, "communication" with the British Soul would become ever more difficult. It may well be that Ulster Protestant exasperation with Westminster will, after all, alter the fulcrum point far more than Irish Republican exasperation – for it is one thing to confront an enemy, it is another to be stabbed in the back by "friends."

No human being can know the future with certainty, however inspired or informed. But one thing is sure. A real and profound knowledge of the past is vital to a real and lasting comprehension of the present. Things in Ireland have changed; but not as much as one might think; relations between England and Ireland have changed – but to what degree? A deep study of this marvelous work by Chesterton will give birth to mature fruit if approached in the right way. May God permit us to hope that such fruit will include the restoration of Ireland, the Land of Saints and Scholars, and the reawakening of England, Our Lady's Dowry.

The Directors
IHS Press
December 29, 2002
Feast of St. Thomas Becket

"We want such widely diffused prosperity that the Irish people will not be crushed by destitution into living 'the lives of the beasts.' Neither must they be obliged, owing to an unsound economic condition, to spend all their power of both mind and body in an effort to satisfy the bodily needs alone. The uses of wealth are to provide good health, comfort, moderate luxury, and to give the freedom which comes from the possession of these things."

—Michael Collins (1890–1922)

Introduction

In early 1918 a strange couple came to Ireland on a mission as strange as themselves. One was a bachelor of ascetic temper, a bit prickly, finicky to a fault, an Old Etonian graduate of Oxford, included in whose otherwise conventional upper-class upbringing was time spent in a ranch in Wyoming. Without family but with sufficient private income to do much as he pleased, he had dedicated his life to the promotion of rural co-operatives in Ireland, preaching the cause with visionary zeal. An Isaiah of the country creamery, a John the Baptist of the combine harvester, he foresaw a country made beautiful by small farmers working together to transform their shared landscape. Independent but honorably reliant on the efforts of others, proud of their plots but not jealous of the plots of their neighbors, they would renew the face of the earth, becoming (as the second member of the party would later describe them) a multitude of men standing on their own feet because they were standing on their own land. This prophet of rural regeneration was Sir Horace Plunkett and his name is still held in affection in Ireland today. Plunkett's companion, while endorsing this dream, could not have been more different in appearance or personality. Large, affable, disorganized, fond of beer, he came to Ireland by way of Saint Paul's school, the Slade, and several pubs in between. A journalist of genius (indeed a genius pure and simple) he was an English patriot who saw no contradiction – indeed the opposite – in arguing the cause of Ireland. In column after column he urged his countrymen to be decent in their dealings with the island to the west. He offered no defense of a history written, for the most part, in sorrow and blood. He was, of course, G.K. Chesterton: a man, as Plunkett quirkily put it, of "great personal magnitude." Out of his visit emerged *Irish Impressions*, one of the sharpest books ever written by an Englishman about Ireland and easily the most significant result of an eccentric and endearing trip.

Irish Impressions may be read and enjoyed as a free-standing volume. Its meaning reveals itself without much need for explanation or historical context. Certainly it is one of Chesterton's most relaxed and engaging books, full of good jokes and insights, affectionate towards Ireland and the Irish but not adulatory, playful and paradoxical but not predictably so. It was not a literary exercise, a case of Ireland, as it were, being given the Chestertonian treatment. Yet context *is* important. To read the book without it is to miss much of its subtlety. *Irish Impressions* will only make an impression – will only seem truly impressive – if we know its time and place, the world in which the word was made. As with many of Chesterton's books, it was an occasional piece that far surpassed the occasion that prompted it.

Why, then, did Plunkett and GKC come to Ireland? They hoped to persuade Irishmen to enlist on behalf of the Allied cause in the Great War, which was then moving rapidly towards its climax. This was an appeal that worked once before. John Redmond, leader of the Irish Parliamentary Party at Westminster, tried it in 1914, persuading thousands of his countrymen that small, Catholic Belgium was worth defending in the face of Prussian Protestantism. Although prompted by genuine pity for the Belgian plight, there was also political calculation behind the appeal. Redmond believed that the defense of a small nation could only help the cause of Ireland. Joining the colors would help to ensure "Home Rule," that is to say, the long-standing demand for an Irish parliament sitting in Dublin. But that was 1914. By 1918 the world had changed utterly. No-one could have known in those early days and weeks that the war would prove so dreadful and so calamitous. The carnage of Passchendaele and the Somme shocked the world. It also destroyed (a relatively minor consequence, to be sure) the political career of John Redmond. In such circumstance, further Irish involvement in the trenches was almost unthinkable. But there was another, more immediate factor that argued against enlistment: the Easter Rising of 1916 and its bloody aftermath. Chesterton, for once lacking acuity, regarded this rebellion simply as "the Dublin riot." In fact, it was enormously consequential. The center of Ireland's capital was reduced to rubble, the rebel leaders were executed, the cause of constitutional nationalism at Westminster was dealt a blow from which it never recovered, and violent Irish republicanism (a tradition dating at least from the United Irish rebellion of 1798) was given a new lease of life. The leaders of the rising had no interest in Redmondite Home Rule which they considered, with some justice, a watered down devolution that would have kept Ireland in a state of continued colonial dependency and stunted nationhood. A fully-fledged Irish Republic was their goal and (for a week or so in 1916) their nominal achievement. With Irish and English public opinion so far apart, could much hope have been held out for the success of a recruiting campaign in early 1918? Chesterton and Plunkett must have known that their task was forlorn. Yet on they rode, tilting cheerfully at windmills: a couple of Quixotes destined magnificently to fail. Rarely has so genial a book been produced in circumstances so uncongenial.

For all that, the good humor of *Irish Impressions* is not a pose. Chesterton had reasons to be cheerful, not least the simple pleasure of coming to Ireland for the first time and seeing for himself a country he had long considered a model Christian nation. Until 1918 he knew Ireland only indirectly, mainly through the company of Irish intellectuals and politicians living in London: the painter John B. Yeats and his son, Willie, better known to history as W.B. Yeats; the playwright John Millington Synge; the literary hostess Lady Gregory; the MP John Redmond. They were a variegated bunch, in some ways typically Irish (lovers of language, at once serious and comical, undeniably exotic against a staid English background) and in other ways untypical (mostly Protestant, more or less professional, people who had never dug a potato in their lives). After their own fashion these London Irish convinced Chesterton of a few truths about the country that produced them. The first was that Irish intellectuals were indeed intelligent, some of them supremely so. Chesterton considered John Yeats the best talker he ever met; his son was almost as good. Synge was a dramatist of real originality, perhaps even genius; Redmond could speak with more than ordinary passion and eloquence. These men showed him that words were the national pastime, perhaps the national failing, providing a pleasure so great that all other activity came distantly second to it. Moreover, the talking occurred in a home. Nothing impressed Chesterton so much about the Irish as their attachment to kitchen and hearth. He liked to speak of the "drama of the home," of the fact that humanly important things – birth, rearing, death – all took place in a domestic setting. That was why, he said, those most revolutionary about the state were most conservative about the family. They recognized the deeper implications of the demand for national self-determination. A parliament in Dublin was not an end in itself, they understood, but a means towards some greater goal, its real purpose being to allow Irishmen to be *Irish*, not imitation Englishmen. This was rarely grasped by English promoters of Home Rule, especially Gladstonian Liberals with their high-minded, rational, progressive, curiously solipsistic view of the world. Too preoccupied with the Irish Question, they missed the Irish Answer. And that answer, Chesterton said, was so obvious as to go almost unsaid. The demand for Home Rule was really a demand for the rule of the home. It was an argument that faith and family come first. It was an assertion that the House of Commons should promote common houses. It was an appeal that the mother of parliaments should have some interest in mothers.

The charm of *Irish Impressions* thus derives in part from Chesterton's discovery that Irish in Ireland were no different from the Irish he first encountered in England: talkative, humorous, familial, frequently absurd. They could also be cruel. There was romance in Chesterton's portrayal but also realism, an awareness of national vices (long memory, begrudgery, occasional unkindness) as well as virtues (charm, thoughtfulness, imagination). This recognition of Irish flaws seems to lend verisimilitude to the book, a sense of balance. Yet it is not always convincing. A standard criticism of Chesterton (one, however, that misses a larger point) is that his writing is full of types and tropes, stock figures designed to illustrate a moral rather than complex human beings capable of ambiguous action or motive. Consider his account of Ulster Protestants. These were the men, as he put it in *The Flying Inn*, who live in "black Belfast…/ and think we're burning witches when we're only burning weeds." It contains good things, to be sure, but it is also procrustean, schematic, and too trite to be taken seriously. Ulster stood as an objective correlative, a synecdoche for too many troubles: the insolence of industrialism, the coldness of Calvinism, the corruption of the party political game, the dangers, of all things, of Prussianism. Of course, Chesterton's was a figurative imagination, more at home with symbol and allegory than dry reportage. Still, even his realism – his description of the hard and flinty Presbyterian mind – is curiously unreal. It is literary device, little else. More reportage and less romance might have done the argument a lot of good.

Yet this is to cavil. Even when the book seems to offer harsh judgments, geniality keeps breaking through. Why? Is it because of Chesterton's irrepressible good humor, his splendid optimism? Perhaps. Yet there was a reason more immediate than that. Chesterton and Plunkett may have made improbable recruiting sergeants; Ireland may have been too far gone in republicanism to rediscover Home Rule as a political crusade; the Orange card may have been thrown once too often. Those difficulties notwithstanding, Chesterton's vision of Ireland was vindicated by the central fact he reported in the book – a fact so great he thought it little short of a miracle, another resurrection. The land of Ireland, he was able to report in triumph, was once again owned by the people of Ireland. Two parliamentary measures had turned the Irish tenant into a landowner: Ashbourne's Land Act of 1885 and Wyndham's Land Act of 1903. Between 1906 and 1908 alone, more than 100,000 renters had been able to buy their own farms. By 1914 nearly three-quarters of Ireland's farmers owned the land they farmed. No wonder Chesterton considered George Wyndham, author of the 1903 Act, the finest statesman he had ever known. "At the price of nobody knows what pain and patience," amidst the ruins of a decadent parliamentary system, he alone established a free peasantry in Ireland. It was because of his efforts that Home Rule had become a social and economic reality. All that awaited was that it should become a political reality as well. If ever the case for distributism needed to be made, Ireland, and Wyndham, made it. What Chesterton called "the poetry of private property" had come alive in a land that almost died for lack of it. That was the real Easter Rising, the true greatness of Ireland. "The meaning of these green and solid things before me is that it is not a ghost that has risen from the grave... It is a miracle more marvelous than the resurrection of the dead. It is the resurrection of the body." The wearing of the greens, he joked, was better than the wearing of the green. Or, to put the matter slightly differently, in Ireland (and in all sane places) cabbages are kings.

Yet that was not the only news Chesterton reported in 1918. It was true that a land and a landscape had been transformed, vindicating not only the value but also the very possibility of small proprietorships and the family life that such proprietorships help to sustain. Passages from *Irish Impressions* could be taken from *The Outline of Sanity*, Chesterton's later defense of private property on a human scale. All this may be granted. But the story was even deeper. A people had been made whole by the recovery of their land: they had also been made holy. This was true in a double sense. Chesterton saw sacramentality in the life of the land. Sowing and reaping, cycles and seasons, are the stuff of creation itself. Incarnational truths are revealed by rows of beans and plots of potatoes. Physical things have metaphysical meaning. They are glimpses – sometimes brief, sometimes blinding – of an unseen Maker. And the work of the land, the co-operation grower with Creator, is good in other ways. In a real sense, a man does not cultivate land: the land cultivates him. It teaches him patience, thankfulness, humility. It offers him a chance to provide for himself and his family. It reveals new beauties every day. It is solace for the soul.

And there was a second way in which the people of Ireland had been made holy by the return of their land. The recovery of property was a sign and symbol, Chesterton thought, of the survival of Christianity itself. Throughout their history the Irish never wavered in fidelity to the gospel, clinging to it the more firmly as the darkness deepened and the tides threatened to carry them away. That faithfulness was a kind of sermon, a lesson to others. If Christianity was not meant to survive, if the cross was not meant to triumph, Chesterton was at a loss to know why it had survived in Ireland.

This is why *Irish Impressions* is significant beyond the occasion that prompted it. That is why it also should be read along with Chesterton's other great Irish work, *Christendom in Dublin*, published in 1932 after the Eucharistic Congress of that year. The first book is a spirited account of a spirited journey, a record of a good-hearted jaunt

Introduction

with talk and laughter and fellowship along the way. The second book is mellow, reflective, somehow autumnal in its sense that Ireland's journey to nationhood had been completed as his own life was nearing its end. But whatever their surface differences both books are essentially soul odysseys, indeed the odysseys of two souls – Chesterton's and Ireland's. Author and country were well matched. He never ceased to delight that in an age of rationalism, Ireland remained religious. In an era of eugenics, it favored family life. In a time of trusts, it trusted the farm. In a world that worshipped wealth, it preferred frugality. When greatness and grandiosity were all the rage, it preferred a beautiful smallness – the life of the field, the village, the story by the fire. Those truths are not less true for having been expressed, with wit and grace, almost a century ago.

Dermot Quinn
Department of History
Seton Hall University, New Jersy, USA

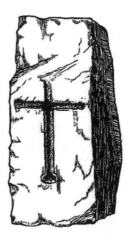

Chronology of Irish History

432 AD   St. Patrick arrives in Ireland, marking the beginning of a serious effort to convert the Irish to Catholicism.

1014   Battle of Clontarf. Ireland's greatest king, Brian Boru, decisively crushes the Viking invaders.

1170   The English-Norman invasion of Ireland. Marks the beginning of the eight-century long struggle to end English occupation of the island of Ireland.

1556   Queen Elizabeth I of England begins the Plantation. Protestants, mainly Scottish Presbyterians, are transferred to Ireland to dominate and outbreed the native Irish.

1649   Oliver Cromwell, English Puritan leader and regicide, arrives in Ireland and begins to massacre Catholics. The atrocity at the city of Drogheda becomes a by-word for English oppression, and remains foremost in the Irish memory even today.

1690   Battle of the Boyne. The Stuart and Catholic cause is lost to the Protestant Dutchman, William of Orange, invited to take the Crown of England by the Protestant rich.

1691   The Treaty of Limerick is signed. The remaining Irish Stuart troops are given free passage to France. It is the effective departure of the Irish nobility, and becomes known as the "flight of the wild geese."

1692   Catholics are excluded from office for the first time.

1695   Penal Laws are introduced, depriving Catholics of their civil rights.

1829   Catholic emancipation. Limited restoration of civil rights to Catholics by Parliament as a result of the leadership of Daniel O'Connell.

1845   The first year of the Irish Famine. Led to the death and exile of over one third of the Irish population. The callousness of the English government in refusing to help the Irish practically – when the whole country was littered with corpses – is another event fresh in Irish memory.

1877 Irish nationalist leader, Michael Davitt, founds the *Land League*. Marks the beginning of a new phase in the struggle of the Irish to recapture the ownership of the land of Ireland.

1893 Irish Protestant Douglas Hyde founds the *Gaelic League* to revive Irish culture. It is a resounding success.

1916 The Easter Rising, led by James Connolly and Patrick Pearse. The the Irish Republic is proclaimed, leading to terrible repression, with some 1,400 Irish republicans facing over 14,000 well armed British troops, backed by artillery. The Rising is crushed after five bloody days, but continues the Irish tradition since the Norman days of having a military rising in every generation.

1919–21 The War of Irish Independence. Led principally by Michael Collins, it replaces the failed tactics of the past, which involved direct confrontation with superior English military forces, and institutes urban and guerilla warfare. It leads to an offer from the British for peace talks as their position becomes untenable. This period also witnesses the emergence of the IRA.

1922 A Treaty establishes the Irish Free State in 26 of Ireland's 32 counties. The Free State becomes the Republic of Ireland several decades later. However, the partition of the country, creating the statelet "Northern Ireland" under Protestant domination, effected the abandonment of the Catholics in the Northeast of the country, and led to dissension in Irish Republican ranks. The Anti-Treaty IRA fought a Civil War with the Free Staters from 1922 to 1923, but were eventually forced to surrender. They continued the struggle in the North of Ireland for a 32 County Republic, becoming the historical point of reference for the modern IRA.

"Englishmen believed in Irish decay even when they were large-minded enough to lament it.... This sight of things sustaining, and a beauty that nourishes and does not merely charm, was a premonition of practicality in the miracle of modern Ireland. It is a miracle more marvellous than the resurrection of the dead. It is the resurrection of the body."

I. Two Stones in a Square

HEN I HAD FOR THE FIRST TIME CROSSED ST. George's Channel, and for the first time stepped out of a Dublin hotel on to St. Stephen's Green, the first of all my impressions was that of a particular statue, or rather portion of a statue. I left many traditional mysteries already in my track, but they did not trouble me as did this random glimpse or vision. I have never understood why the Channel is called St. George's Channel; it would seem more natural to call it St. Patrick's Channel, since the great missionary did almost certainly cross that unquiet sea and look up at those mysterious mountains. And though I should be enchanted, in an abstract artistic sense, to imagine St. George sailing towards the sunset, flying the silver and scarlet colours of his cross, I cannot in fact regard that journey as the most fortunate of the adventures of that flag. Nor, for that matter, do I know why the Green should be called St. Stephen's Green, nor why the parliamentary enclosure at Westminster is also connected with the first of the martyrs; unless it is because St. Stephen[1] was killed with stones. The stones, piled together to make modern political buildings, might perhaps be regarded as a cairn, or heap of missiles, marking the place of the murder of a witness to the truth. And while it seems unlikely that St. Stephen was pelted with statues as well as stones, there are undoubtedly statues that might well kill a Christian at sight. Among these graven stones, from which the saints suffer, I should certainly include some of those figures in frock coats standing opposite St. Stephen's Westminster. There are many such statues in Dublin also; but the one with which I am concerned was at first partially veiled from me. And the veil was at least as symbolic as the vision.

I saw what seemed the crooked hind legs of a horse on a pedestal and deduced an equestrian statue, in the somewhat bloated fashion of the early eighteenth century equestrian statues. But the figure, from where I stood, was wholly hidden in the tops of trees growing round it in a ring; masking it with leafy curtains or draping it with leafy banners. But they were green banners, that wave and glittered all about it in the sunlight; and the face they hid was the face of an English king. Or rather, to speak more correctly, a German king.

When laws can stay...it was impossible that an old rhyme should not run in my head, and words that appealed to the everlasting revolt of the green things of the earth.... "And when the leaves in summer time their colour dare not show."[2] The rhyme seemed to reach me out of remote times and find arresting fulfilment, like a prophecy; it was impossible not to feel that I had seen an omen. I was conscious vaguely of a vision of green garlands hung on gray stone; and the wreaths were living and growing, and the stone was dead. Something in the simple substances and elemental colours, in the white sunlight, and the sombre and even secret image held the mind for a moment in the midst of all the moving city, like a sign given in a dream. I was told that the figure was that of one of the first Georges; but indeed I seemed to know already that it was the White Horse of Hanover that had thus grown gray with Irish weather or green with Irish foliage. I knew only too well, already, that the George who had really crossed the Channel was not the saint. This was one of those German princes whom the English aristocracy used when it made the English domestic polity aristocratic and the English foreign policy German. Those Englishmen who think the Irish are pro-German, or those Irishmen who think the Irish ought to be pro-German, would presumably expect the Dublin populace to have hung the statue of this German deliverer with national flowers and nationalist flags. For some reason, however, I found no traces of Irish tributes round the pedestal of the Teutonic horsemen. I wondered how many people in the last fifty years had ever cared about it, or even been conscious of their own carelessness. I wonder how many have ever troubled to look at it, or even troubled not to look at it. If it fell down,

Two Stones in a Square 27

I wonder whether anybody would put it up again. I do not know; I only know that Irish gardeners, or some such Irish humorists, had planted trees in a ring round that prancing equestrian figure; trees that had, so to speak, sprung up and choked him, making him more unrecognisable than a Jack-in-the-Green. Jack or George had vanished; but the Green remained.

About a stone's throw from this calamity in stone there stood, at the corner of a gorgeously coloured flower-walk, a bust evidently by a modern sculptor, with modern symbolic ornament surmounted by the fine falcon face of the poet Mangan,[3] who dreamed and drank and died, a thoughtless and thriftless outcast, in the darkest of the Dublin streets around that place. This individual Irishman really was what we were told that all Irishmen were, hopeless, heedless, irresponsible, impossible, a tragedy of failure. And yet it seemed to be his head that was lifted and not hidden; the gay flowers only showed up this graven image as the green leaves shut out the other; everything around him seemed bright and busy, and told rather of a new time. It was clear that modern men did stop to look at *him*; indeed modern men had stayed there long enough to make him a monument. It was almost certain that if his monument fell down it really would be put up again. I think it very likely there would be competition among advanced modern artistic schools of admitted crankiness and unimpeachable lunacy; that somebody would want to cut out a Cubist[4] Mangan in a style less of stone than of bricks; or to set up a Vorticist[5] Mangan, like a frozen whirlpool, to terrify the children playing in that flowery lane. For when I afterwards went into the Dublin Art Club,[6] or mixed generally in the stimulating society of the intellectuals of the Irish capital, I found a multitude of things which moved both my admiration and amusement. Perhaps the best thing of all was that it was the one society that I have seen where the intellectuals were intellectual. But nothing pleased me more than the fact that even Irish art was taken with a certain Irish pugnacity; as if there could be street fights about aesthetics as there once were about theology. I could almost imagine an appeal for pikes to settle a point about art needlework, or a suggestion of dying on the barricades for a difference about bookbinding. And I could still more easily imagine a sort of ultra-civilized civil war round the half-restored bust of poor Mangan. But it was in a yet plainer and more popular sense that I felt that bust to be the sign of a new world, where the statue of Royal George was only the ruin of an old one. And though I have since seen many much more complex, and many decidedly contradictory things in Ireland, the allegory of those two stone images in that public garden has remained in my memory, and has not been reversed. The Glorious Revolution, the great Protestant Deliverer,[7] the Hanoverian Succession,[8] these things were the very pageant and apotheosis of success. The Whig[9] aristocrat was not merely victorious; it was as a victor that he asked for victory. The thing was fully expressed in all the florid and insolent statuary of the period, in all those tumid horsemen in Roman uniform and rococo periwigs shown as prancing in perpetual motion down shouting streets to their triumphs; only today the streets are empty and silent, and the horse stands still. Of such a kind was the imperial figure round which the ring of trees had risen, like great green fans to soothe a sultan or great green curtains to guard him. But it was in a sort of mockery that his pavilion was thus painted with the colour of his conquered enemies. For the king was dead behind his curtains, his voice will be heard no more, and no man will even wish to hear it, while the world endures. The dynastic eighteenth century is dead if anything is dead; and these idols at least are only stones. But only a few yards away, the stone that the builders rejected is really the head of a corner, standing at the corner of a new pathway, coloured and crowded with children and with flowers.

That, I suspect, is the paradox of Ireland in the modern world. Everything that was thought progressive as a prancing horse has come to a standstill. Everything that was thought decadent as a dying drunkard has risen from the dead. All that seemed to have reached a *cul de sac* has turned the corner, and stands at the opening of a new road. All that thought itself on a pedestal has found itself up a tree. And that is why those two chance stones seem to me to stand like graven images on either side of the gateway by which a man enters Ireland. And yet I had not left the same small enclosure till I had seen one other sight which was even more symbolic than the flowers near the foot of the poet's pedestal. A few yards beyond the

Mangan bust was a model plot of vegetables, like a kitchen garden with no kitchen or house attached to it, planted out in a patchwork of potatoes, cabbages and turnips, to prove how much could be done with an acre. And I realized as in a vision that all over the new Ireland that patch is repeated like a pattern; and where there is a real kitchen garden there is also a real kitchen; and it is not a communal kitchen. It is more typical even than the poet and the flowers; for these flowers are also food, and this poetry is also property; property which, when properly distributed, is the poetry of the average man. It was only afterwards that I could realize all the realities to which this accident corresponded; but even this little public experiment, at the first glance, had something of the meaning of a public monument. It was this which the earth itself had reared against the monstrous image of the German monarch; and I might have called this chapter Cabbages and Kings.

My life is passed in making bad jokes and seeing them turn into true prophecies. In the little town in South Bucks, where I live, I remember some talk of appropriate ceremonies in connection with the work of sending vegetables to the Fleet. There was a suggestion that some proceedings should end with "God Save the King," an amendment by someone (of a more naval turn of mind) to substitute "Rule Britannia"; and the opposite of one individual, claiming to be of Irish extraction, who loudly refused to lend a voice to either. Whatever I retain, in such rural scenes, of the frivolity of Fleet Street led me to suggest that we could all join in singing "The Wearing of the Greens." But I have since discovered that this remark, like other typical utterances of the village idiot, was in truth inspired; and was a revelation and a vision from across the sea, a vision of what was really being done, not by the village idiots but by the village wise men. For the whole miracle of modern Ireland might well be summed up in the simple change from the word "green" to the word "greens." Nor would it be true to say that the first is poetical and the second practical. For the green tree is quite as poetical as a green flag; and no one in touch with history doubts that the waving of the green flag has been very useful to the growing of the green tree. But I shall have to touch upon all such controversial topics later, for those to whom such statements are still controversial. Here I would only begin by recording a first impression as vividly coloured and patchy as a modernist picture; a square of green things growing where they are least expected; the new vision of Ireland. The discovery, for most Englishmen, will be like touching the trees of a faded tapestry, and finding the forest alive and full of birds. It will be as if, on some dry urn or dreary column, figures which had already begun to crumble magically began to move and dance. For culture as well as mere caddishness assumed the decay of these Celtic or Catholic things; there were artists sketching the ruins as well as trippers picnicking in them; and it was not the only evidence that a final silence had fallen on the harp of Tara,[10] that it did not play "Tararaboomdeay."[11] Englishmen believed in Irish decay even when they were large-minded enough to lament it. It might be said that those who were most penitent because the thing was murdered, were most convinced that it was killed. The meaning of these green and solid things before me is that it is not a ghost that has risen from the grave. A flower, like a flag, might be little more than a ghost; but a fruit has that sacramental solidity which in all mythologies belongs not to a ghost, but to a god. This sight of things sustaining, and a beauty that nourishes and does not merely charm, was a premonition of practicality in the miracle of modern Ireland. It is a miracle more marvellous than the resurrection of the dead. It is the resurrection of the body.

II. The Root of Reality

HE ONLY EXCUSE OF LITERATURE IS TO MAKE things new; and the chief misfortune of journalism is that it has to make them old. What is hurried has to be hackneyed. Suppose a man has to write on a particular subject, let us say America; if he has a day to do it in, it is possible that, in the last afterglow of sunset, he may have discovered at least one thing which he himself really thinks about America. It is conceivable that somewhere under the evening star he may have a new idea, even about the new world. If he has only half an hour in which to write, he will just have time to consult an encyclopaedia and vaguely remember the latest leading articles. The encyclopaedia will be only about a decade out of date; the leading articles will be aeons out of date – having been written under similar conditions of modern rush. If he has only a quarter of an hour in which to write about America, he may be driven in mere delirium and madness to call her his Gigantic Daughter in the West, to talk of the feasibility of Hands Across the Sea, or even to call himself an Anglo-Saxon, when he might as well call himself a Jute. But whatever debasing banality be the effect of business scurry in criticism, it is but one example of a truth that can be tested in twenty fields of experience. If a man must get to Brighton as quickly as possible, he can get there quickest by travelling on rigid rails on a recognized route. If he has time and money for motoring, he will still use public roads; but he will be surprised to find how many public roads look as new and quiet as private roads. If he has time enough to walk, he may find for himself a string of fresh footpaths, each one a fairytale. This law of the leisure needed for the awakening of wonder applies, indeed, to things superficially

familiar as well as to things superficially fresh. The chief case for old enclosures and boundaries is that they enclose a space in which new things can always be found later, like live fish within the four corners of a net. The chief charm of having a home that is secure is having leisure to feel it as strange.

I have often done the little I could to correct the stale trick of taking things for granted: all the more because it is not even taking them for granted. It is taking them without gratitude; that is, emphatically as not granted. Even one's own front door, released by one's own latchkey, should not only open inward on things familiar, but outward on things unknown. Even one's own domestic fireside should be wild as well as domesticated; for nothing could be wilder than fire. But if this light of the higher ignorance should shine even on familiar places, it should naturally shine most clearly on the roads of a strange land. It would be well if a man could enter Ireland really knowing that he knows nothing about Ireland; if possible, not even the name of Ireland. The misfortune is that most men know the name too well, and the thing too little. This book would probably be a better book, as well as a better joke, if I were to call the island throughout by some name like Atlantis, and only reveal on the last page that I was referring to Ireland. Englishmen would see a situation of great interest, objects with which they could feel considerable sympathy, and opportunities of which they might take considerable advantage, if only they would really look at the place plain and straight, as they would at some entirely new island, with an entirely new name, discovered by that seafaring adventure which is the real romance of England. In short, the Englishman might do something with it, if he would only treat it as an object in front of him, and not as a subject or story left behind him. There will be occasion later to say all that should be said of the need of studying the Irish story. But the Irish story is one thing and what is called the Irish Question quite another; and in a purely practical sense the best thing the stranger can do is to forget the Irish Question and look at the Irish. If he looked at them simply and steadily, as he would look at the natives of an entirely new nation with a new name, he would become conscious of a very strange but entirely solid fact. He would become conscious of it, as a man in a fairy tale might become conscious that he had crossed the border of fairyland, by such a trifle as a talking cow or a haystack walking about on legs.

For the Irish Question has never been discussed in England. Men have discussed Home Rule;[12] but those who advocated it most warmly, and as I think wisely, did not even know what the Irish meant by Home. Men have talked about Unionism;[13] but they have never even dared to propose Union. A Unionist ought to mean a man who is not even conscious of the boundary of the two countries; who can walk across the frontier of fairyland, and not even notice the walking haystack. As a fact, the Unionist always shoots at the haystack; though he never hits it. But the limitation is not limited to Unionists; as I have already said, the English Radicals have been quite as incapable of going to the root of the matter. Half the case for Home Rule was that Ireland could not be trusted to the English Home Rulers. They also, to recur to the parable, have been unable to take the talking cow by the horns; for I need hardly say that the talking cow is an Irish bull. What has been the matter with their Irish politics was simply that they were English politics. They discussed the Irish Question; but they never seriously contemplated the Irish Answer. That is, the Liberal was content with the negative truth, that the Irish should not be prevented from having the sort of law they liked. But the Liberal seldom faced the positive truth, about what sort of law they would like. He instinctively avoided the very imagination of this; for the simple reason that the law the Irish would like is as remote from what is called Liberal as from what is called Unionist. Nor has the Liberal ever embraced it in his broadest liberality, nor the Unionist ever absorbed it into his most complete unification. It remains outside us altogether, a thing to be stared at like a fairy cow; and by far the wisest English visitor is he who will simply stare at it. Sooner or later he will see what it means; which is simply this: that whether it be a case for coercion or emancipation (and it might be used either way) the fact is that a free Ireland would not only not be what we call lawless, but might not even be what we call free. So far from being an anarchy, it would be an orderly and even conservative civilization – like the Chinese. But it would be a civilization so fundamentally different from our own, that our own Liberals would differ from it as much as our own Conservatives. The fair question for an Englishman is whether that fundamental difference would make division dangerous; it has already made union impossible. Now in turning over these notes of so brief a visit, suffering from all the stale scurry of my journalistic trade, I have been in doubt between a chronological and a logical order of events. But I have decided in favour of logic, of the high light that really revealed the picture, and by which I firmly believe that everything else should be seen. And if any one were to ask me what was the sight that struck me most in Ireland, both as strange and significant, I should know what to reply. I saw it long after I had seen the Irish cities, had felt something of the brilliant bitterness of Dublin and the stagnant optimism of Belfast; but I put it first here because I am certain that with it all the rest is meaningless; that it lies behind all politics, enormous and silent, as the great hills lie beyond Dublin.

I was moving in a hired motor down a road in the North-West, towards the middle of that rainy autumn. I was not moving very fast; because the progress was slowed down to a solemn procession by crowds of families with their cattle and livestock going to the market beyond; which things also are an allegory. But what struck my mind and stuck in it was this; that all down one side of the road, as far as we went, the harvest was gathered in neatly and safely; and all down the other side of the road it was rotting in the rain. Now the side where it was safe was a string of small plots worked by peasant proprietors, as petty by our standards as a row of the cheapest villas. The land on which all the harvest was wasted was the land of a large modern estate. I asked why the landlord was later with his harvesting than the peasants; and I was told rather vaguely that there had been strikes and similar labour troubles. I did not go into the rights of the matter; but the point here is that, whatever they were, the moral is the same. You may curse the cruel Capitalist landlord or you may rave at the ruffianly Bolshevist strikers; but you must admit that between them they had produced a stoppage, which the peasant proprietorship a few yards off did not produce. You might support either where they conflicted, but you could not deny the sense in which they had combined, and combined to prevent what a few rustics across the road could combine to produce. For all that we in England agree about and disagree about, all for which we fight and all from which we differ, our darkness and our light, our heaven and hell, were there on the left side of the road. On the right side of the road lay something so different that we do not even differ from it. It may be that Trusts are rising like towers of gold and iron, overshadowing the earth and shutting out the sun; but they are only rising on the left side of the road. It may be that Trade Unions are laying labyrinths of international insurrection, cellars stored with the dynamite of a merely destructive democracy; but all that international maze lies to the left side of the road. Employment and unemployment are there; Marx[14] and the Manchester School[15] are there. The left side of the road may even go through amazing transformations of its own; its story may stride across abysses of anarchy; but it will never step across the road. The landlord's estate may become a sort of Morris[16] Utopia, organized communally by Socialists, or more probably by Guild Socialists. It may (as I fear is much more likely) pass through the stage of an employer's model village to the condition of an old pagan slave-estate. But the peasants across the road would not only refuse the Servile State, but would quite as resolutely refuse the Utopia. Europe may seem to be torn from end to end by the blast of a Bolshevist trumpet, sundering the bourgeois from the proletarian; but the peasant across the road is neither a bourgeois nor a proletarian. England may seem to be rent by an irreconcilable rivalry between Capital and Labour; but the peasant across the road is both a capitalist and a labourer. He is several other curious things; including the man who got his crops in first; who was literally the first in the field.

To an Englishman, especially a Londoner, this was like walking to the corner of a London street and finding the policeman in rags, with a patch on his trousers and a smudge on his face; but the crossing-sweeper wearing a single eyeglass and a suit fresh from a West End tailor. In fact, it was nearly as surprising as a walking haystack or a talking cow. What was generally dingy, dilatory, and down-at-heels was here comparatively tidy and timely; what was orderly and organized was belated and abandoned. For it must be sharply realized that the peasant proprietors succeeded here, not only because they were really proprietors, but because they were only peasants. It was *because* they were on a small scale that they were a great success. It was because they were too poor to have servants that they grew rich in spite of strikers. It was, so far as it went, the flattest possible contradiction to all that is said in England, both by Collectivists and Capitalists, about the efficiency of the great organization. For insofar as it had failed, it had actually failed, not only through being great, but through being organized. On the left side of the road the big machine had stopped working, *because* it was a big machine. The small men were still working, because they were not machines. Such were the strange relations of the two things, that the stars in their courses fought against Capitalism; that the very clouds rolling over that rocky valley warred for its pigmies against its giants. The rain falls alike on the just and the unjust; yet here it had not fallen alike on the rich and poor. It had fallen to the destruction of the rich.

Now I do, as a point of personal opinion, believe that the right side of the road was really the right side of the road. That is, I believe it represented the right side of the question; that these little pottering peasants had got hold of the true secret, which is missed by both Capitalism and Collectivism. But I am not here urging my own preferences on my own countrymen; and I am not concerned primarily to point out that this is an argument against Capitalism and Collectivism. What I do point out is that it is the fundamental argument against Unionism. Perhaps it is, on that ultimate level, the only argument against Unionism; which is probably why it is never used against Unionists. I mean, of course, that it was never really used against English Unionists by English Home Rulers, in the recriminations of that Irish Question which was really an English Question. The essential demanded of that question was merely that it should be an open question; a thing rather like an open wound. Modern industrial society is fond of problems, and therefore not at all fond of solutions. A consideration of those who really have understood this fundamental fact will be sufficient to show how confusing and useless are the mere party labels in the matter. George Wyndham[17]

The Root of Reality

was a Unionist who was deposed because he was a Home Ruler. Sir Horace Plunkett[18] is a Unionist who is trusted because he is a Home Ruler. By far the most revolutionary piece of Nationalism that was ever really effected for Ireland was effected by Wyndham, who was an English Tory squire. And by far the most brutal and brainless piece of Unionism that was ever imposed on Ireland was imposed in the name of the Radical theory of Free Trade, when the Irish juries brought in verdicts of wilful murder against Lord John Russell.[19] I say this to show that my sense of a reality is quite apart from the personal accident that I have myself always been a Radical in English politics, as well as a Home Ruler in Irish politics. But I say it even more in order to reaffirm that the English have first to forget all their old formulae and look at a new fact. It is not a new fact; but it is new to them.

To realize it we must not only go outside the British parties but outside the British Empire, outside the very universe of the ordinary Briton. The real question can be easily stated, for it is as simple as it is large. What is going to happen to the peasantries of Europe, or for that matter of the whole world? It would be far better, as I have already suggested, if we could consider it as a new case of some peasantry in Europe, or somewhere else in the world. It would be far better if we ceased to talk of Ireland and Scotland, and began to talk of Ireland and Serbia. Let us, for the sake of our own mental composure, call this unfortunate people Slovenes. But let us realize that these remote Slovenes are, by the testimony of every truthful traveller, rooted in the habit of private property, and now ripening into a considerable private prosperity. It will often be necessary to remember that the Slovenes are Roman Catholics; and that, with that impatient pugnacity which marks the Slovene temperament, they have often employed violence, but always for the restoration of what they regarded as a reasonable system of private property. Now in a hundred determining districts, of which France is the most famous, this system has prospered. It has its own faults as well as its own merits; but it has prospered. What is going to happen to it? I will here confine myself to saying with the most solid confidence what is not going to happen to it. It is not going to be *really* ruled by Socialists;

and it is not going to be really ruled by merchant princes, like those who ruled Venice or like those who rule England.

It is not merely that England ought not to rule Ireland but that England cannot. It is not merely that Englishmen cannot rule Irishmen, but that merchants cannot rule peasants. It is not so much that we have dealt benefits to England and blows to Ireland. It is that our benefits for England would be blows to Ireland. And this we already began to admit in practice, before we had even dimly begun to conceive it in theory. We do not merely admit it in special laws against Ireland like the Coercion Acts,[20] or special laws in favour of Ireland like the Land Acts;[21] it is admitted even more by specially exempting Ireland than by specially studying Ireland. In other words, whatever else the Unionists want, they do not want to unite; they are not quite so mad as that. I cannot myself conceive any purpose in having one parliament except to pass one law; and one law for England and Ireland is simply something that becomes more insanely impossible every day. If the two societies were stationary, they would be sufficiently separate; but they are both moving rapidly in opposite directions. England may be moving towards a condition which some call Socialism and I call Slavery; but whatever it is, Ireland is speeding farther and farther from it. Whatever it is, the men who manage it will no more be able to manage a European peasantry than the peasants in these mud cabins could manage the Stock Exchange. All attempts, whether imperial or international, to lump these peasants along with some large and shapeless thing called Labour, are part of a cosmopolitan illusion which sees mankind as a map. The world of the International is a pill, as round and as small. It is true that all men want health; but it is certainly not true that all men want the same medicine. Let us allow the cosmopolitan to survey the world from China to Peru; but do not let us allow the chemist to identify Chinese opium and Peruvian bark.

My first parallel about the Slovenes was only a fancy; yet I can give a real parallel from the Slavs which is a fact. It was a fact from my own experience in Ireland; and it exactly illustrates the real international sympathies of peasants. Their internationalism has nothing to do with the International. I had not been in Ireland many hours when several people mentioned to me with considerable excitement some news from the Continent. They were not, strange as it may seem, dancing with joy over the disaster of Caporetto,[22] or glowing with admiration of the Crown Prince. Few really rejoiced in English defeats; and none really rejoiced in German victories. It was news about the Bolsheviks; but it was not the news of how nobly they had given votes to the Russian women, nor of how savagely they had fired bullets into the Russian princesses. It was the news of a check to the Bolshevists; but it was not a glorification of Kerensky[23] or Korniloff,[24] or any of the newspaper heroes who seem to have satisfied us all, so long as their names began with K and nobody knew anything about them. In short, it was nothing that could be found in all our myriad newspaper articles on the subject. I would give an educated Englishman a hundred guesses about what it was; but even if he knew it he would not know what it meant.

It had appeared in the little paper about peasant produce so successfully conducted by Mr. George Russell,[25] the admirable "A.E.," and it was told me eagerly by the poet himself, by a learned and brilliant Jesuit, and by several other people, as the great news from Europe. It was simply the news that the Jewish Socialists of the Bolshevist Government had been attempting to confiscate the peasants' savings in the co-operative banks; and had been forced to desist. And they spoke of it as of a great battle won on the Danube or the Rhine. That is what I mean when I say that these people are of a pattern and belong to a system which cuts across all our own political divisions. They felt themselves fighting the Socialist as fiercely as any Capitalist can feel it. But they not only knew what they were fighting against, but what they were fighting for; which is more than the Capitalist does. I do not know how far modern Europe really shows a menace of Bolshevism, or how far merely a panic of Capitalism. But I know that if any honest resistance has to be offered to mere robbery, the resistance of Ireland will be the most honest, and probably the most important. It may be that international Israel will launch against us out of the East an insane simplification of the unity of Man, as Islam once launched out of the East an insane simplification of the unity of God. If it be so, it is where property is well distributed that it will be well defended. The post of honour will be with those who fight in very truth for their own land. If ever there came such a drive of wild dervishes against us, it would be the chariots and elephants of plutocracy that would roll in confusion and rout; and the squares of the peasant infantry would stand.

Anyhow, the first fact to realize is that we are dealing with a European peasantry; and it would be really better, as I say, to think of it first as a Continental peasantry. There are numberless important inferences from this fact; but there is one point, politically topical and urgent, on which I may well touch here. It will be well to understand about this peasantry something that we generally misunderstand, even about a Continental peasantry. English tourists in France or Italy commonly make the mistake of supposing that the people cheat, because the people bargain, or attempt to bargain. When a peasant asks for tenpence for something that is worth fourpence, the tourist misunderstands the whole problem. He commonly solves it by calling the man a thief and paying the tenpence. There are ten thousand errors in this, beginning with the primary error of an oligarchy, of treating a man as a servant when he feels more like a small squire. The peasant does not choose to receive insults; but he never expected to receive tenpence. A man who understood him would simply suggest twopence, in a calm and courteous manner; and the two would eventually meet in the middle at a perfectly just price. There would not be what we call a fixed price at the beginning, but there would be a very firmly fixed price at the end: that is, the bargain once made would be a sacredly sealed contract. The peasant, so far from cheating, has his own horror of cheating; and certainly his own fury at being cheated. Now in the political bargain with the English, the Irish simply think they have been cheated. They think Home Rule was stolen from them *after* the contract was sealed; and it will be hard for anyone to contradict them. If *"le Roi le veult"*[26] is not a sacred seal on a contract, what is? The sentiment is stronger because the contract was a compromise. Home Rule was the fourpence and not the tenpence; and, in perfect loyalty to the peasant's code of honour, they have now reverted to the tenpence. The Irish have now returned in a reaction of anger to their most extreme demands; *not* because we denied what they demanded, but because we denied what we accepted. As I shall have occasion to note, there are other and wilder elements in the quarrel; but the first fact to remember is that the quarrel began with a bargain, that it will probably have to end with another bargain; and that it will be a bargain with peasants. On the whole, in spite of abominable blunders and bad faith, I think there is still a chance of bargaining, but we must see that there is no chance of cheating. We may haggle like peasants, and remember that their first offer is not necessarily their last. But we must be as honest as peasants; and that is a hard saying for politicians. The great Parnell,[27] a squire who had many of the qualities of a peasant (qualities the English so wildly misunderstood as to think English, when they were really very Irish) converted his people from a Fenianism fiercer than Sinn Fein[28] to a Home Rule more moderate than that which any sane statesmanship would now offer to Ireland. But the peasants trusted Parnell, not because they thought he was asking for it, but because they thought he could get it. Whatever we decide to give to Ireland, we must give it; it is now worse than useless to promise it. I will say here, once and for all, the hardest thing that an Englishman has to say of his impressions of another great European people; that over all those hills and valleys our word is wind, and our bond is waste paper.

But, in any case, the peasantry remains: and the whole weight of the matter is that it will remain. It is much more certain to remain than any of the commercial or colonial systems that will have to bargain with it. We may honestly think that the British Empire is both more liberal and more lasting than the Austrian Empire, or other large political combinations. But a combination like the Austrian Empire could go to pieces, and ten such combinations could go to pieces, before people like the Serbians ceased to desire to be peasants, and to demand to be free peasants. And the British combination, precisely because it is a combination and not a community, is in its nature more lax and liable to real schism than this sort of community, which might almost be called a communion. Any attack on it is like an attempt to abolish grass; which is not only the symbol of it in the old national song, but it is a very true symbol of it in any new philosophic history; a symbol of its equality, its ubiquity, its multiplicity, and its mighty power to return. To fight against grass is to fight against God; we can only so mismanage our own city and our own citizenship that the grass grows in our own streets. And even then it is our streets that will be dead; and the grass will still be alive.

"It is strictly and soberly true that any peasant, in a mud cabin in County Clare, when he names his child Michael, may really have a sense of the presence that smote down Satan, the arms and plumage of the paladin of paradise. I doubt whether it is so overwhelmingly probable that any clerk in any villa on Clapham Common, when he names his son John, has a vision of the holy eagle of the Apocalypse, or even of the mystical cup of the disciple whom Jesus loved."

III. The Family and the Feud

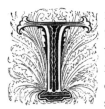HERE WAS AN OLD JOKE OF MY CHILDHOOD, TO the effect that men might be grouped together with reference to their Christian names. I have forgotten the cases then under consideration; but contemporary examples would be sufficiently suggestive today. A ceremonial brotherhood-in-arms between Fr. Bernard Vaughan[29] and Mr. Bernard Shaw seems full of possibilities. I am faintly pleased with the fancy of Mr. Arnold Bennett[30] endeavouring to extract the larger humanities of fiction from the political differences between Mr. Arnold White[31] and Mr. Arnold Lupton.[32] I should pass my own days in the exclusive society of Professor Gilbert Murray[33] and Sir Gilbert Parker;[34] whom I can conceive as differing on some points from each other, and on some points from me. Now there is one odd thing to notice about this old joke; that it might have been taken in a more serious spirit, though in a saner style, in a yet older period. This fantasy of the Victorian Age might easily have been a fact of the Middle Ages. There would have been nothing abnormal in the moral atmosphere of medievalism in some feast or pageant celebrating the fellowship of men who had the same patron saint. It seems mad and meaningless now, because the meaning of Christian names has been lost. They have fallen into a kind of chaos and oblivion which is highly typical of our time. I mean that there are still fashions in them, but no longer reasons for them. For a fashion is a custom without a cause. A fashion is a custom to which men cannot get accustomed; simply because it is without a cause. That is why our industrial societies, touching every topic from the cosmos to the coat collars, are merely swept by a succession of modes which are merely moods. They are customs that fail to be

customary. And so amid all our fashions in Christian names, we have forgotten all that was meant by the custom of Christian names. We have forgotten all the original facts about a Christian name; but, above all, the fact that it was Christian.

Now if we note this process going on in the world of London or Liverpool, we shall see that it has already gone even farther and fared even worse. The surname also is losing its root and therefore its reason. The surname has become as solitary as a nickname. For it might be argued that the first name is meant to be an individual and even isolated thing; but the last name is certainly meant, by all logic and history, to link a man with his human origins, habits or habitation. Historically, it was a word taken from the town he lived in or the trade guild to which he belonged; legally it is still the word on which all questions of legitimacy, succession and testamentary arrangements turn. It is meant to be the corporate name; in that sense it is meant to be the impersonal name, as the other is meant to be the personal name. Yet in the modern mode of industrialism, it is more and more taken in a manner at once lonely and light. Any corporate social system built upon it would seem as much of a joke as the joke about Christian names with which I began. If it would seem odd to require a Thomas to make friends with any other Thomas, it would appear almost as perplexing to insist that any Thompson must love any other Thompson. It may be that Sir Edward Henry,[35] late of the Police Force, does not wish to be confined to the society of Mr. Edward Clodd.[36] But would Sir Edward Henry necessarily seek the society of Mr. O. Henry,[37] entertaining as that society would be? Sir John Barker,[38] founder of the great Kensington emporium, need not specially seek out and embrace Mr. John Masefield;[39] but need he, any more swiftly, precipitate himself into the arms of Mr. Granville Barker?[40] This vista of varieties would lead us far; but it is enough to notice, nonsense apart, that the most ordinary English surnames have become unique in their social significance; they stand for the man rather than the race or the origins. Even when they are most common they are not communal. What we call the family name is not now primarily the name of the family. The family itself, as a corporate conception, has already faded into the background, and is in danger of fading from the background. In short, our Christian names are not the only Christian things that we may lose.

Now the second solid fact which struck me in Ireland (after the success of small property and the *failure* of large organization) was the fact that the family was in a flatly contrary position. All I have said above, in current language, about the whole trend of the modern world, is directly opposite to the whole trend of the modern Irish world. Not only is the Christian name a Christian name; but (what seems still more paradoxical and even pantomimic) the family name is really a family name. Touching the first of the two, it would be easy to trace out some very interesting truths about it, if they did not divert us from the main truth of this chapter; the second great truth about Ireland. People contrasting the "education" of the two countries, or seeking to extend to the one the thing which is called education in the other, might indeed do worse than study the simple problem of the meaning of Christian names. It might dawn at last, even on educationalists, that there is a value in the content as well as the extent of culture; or (in other words), that knowing nine hundred words is not always more important than knowing what some of them mean. It is strictly and soberly true that any peasant, in a mud cabin in County Clare, when he names his child Michael, may really have a sense of the presence that smote down Satan, the arms and plumage of the paladin of paradise. I doubt whether it is so overwhelmingly probable that any clerk in any villa on Clapham Common,[41] when he names his son John, has a vision of the holy eagle of the Apocalypse, or even of the mystical cup of the disciple whom Jesus loved. In the face of that simple fact, I have no doubt about which is the more educated man; and even a knowledge of the *Daily Mail*[42] does not redress the balance. It is often said, and possibly truly, that the peasant named Michael cannot write his own name. But it is quite equally true that the clerk named John cannot read his own name. He cannot read it because it is in a foreign language, and he has never been made to realize what it stands for. He does not know that John means John, as the other man does know that Michael means Michael. In that rigidly realistic sense, the pupil of industrial intellectualism does not even know his own name.

But this is a parenthesis; because the point here is that the man in the street (as distinct from the man in the field) has been separated not only from his private but from his more public description. He has not only forgotten his name, but forgotten his address. In my own view, he is like one of those unfortunate people who wake up with their minds a blank, and cannot therefore find their way home. But whether or no we take this view of the state of things in an industrial society like the English, we must realize firmly that a totally opposite state of things exists in an agricultural society like the Irish. We may put it, if we like, in the form of an unfamiliar and even unfriendly fancy. We may say that the house is greater than the man; that the house is an amiable ogre that runs after and recaptures the man. But the fact is there, familiar or unfamiliar, friendly or unfriendly; and the fact is the family. The family pride is prodigious, though it generally goes along with glowing masses of individual humility. And this family sentiment does attach itself to the family name; so that the very language in which men think is made up of family names. In this the atmosphere is singularly unlike that of England though much more like that of Scotland. Indeed, it will illustrate the impartial recognition of this, apart from any partisan deductions, that it is equally apparent in the place where Ireland and Scotland are supposed to meet. It is equally apparent in Ulster, and even in the Protestant corner of Ulster.

In all the Ulster propaganda I came across, I think the thing that struck me most sharply was one phrase in one Unionist leading article. It was something that might fairly be called Scottish; something which was really even more Irish; but something which could not in the wildest mood be called English, and therefore could not with any rational meaning be called Unionist. Yet it was part of a passionately sincere, and indeed truly human and historic outburst of the politics of the North-East corner, against the politics of the rest of Ireland. Most of us remember that Sir Edward Carson[43] put into the Government a legal friend of his named Campbell;[44] it was at the beginning of the war, and few of us thought anything of the matter except that it was stupid to give posts to Carsonites at the most delicate crisis of the cause in Ireland. Since then, so we also know, the same Campbell has shown himself a sensible man, which I should translate as a practical Home Ruler; but which is anyhow something more than what is generally meant by a Carsonite. I entertain, myself, a profound suspicion that Carson also would very much like to be something more than a Carsonite. But however this may be, his legal friend of whom I speak made an excellent speech, containing some concession to Irish popular sentiment. As might have been expected, there were furious denunciations of him in the Press of the Orange party; but not more furious than might have been found in the *Morning Post*[45] or any Tory paper. Nevertheless, there was one phrase that I certainly never saw in the *Morning Post* or the *Saturday Review*;[46] one phrase I should never expect to see in any English paper, though I might very probably see it in a Scotch paper. It was this sentence, that was read to me from the leading article of a paper in Belfast: "There never was treason yet but a Campbell was at the bottom of it." I give the extract as it was given to me; I am quite conscious of a curious historical paradox about it. A curse against Campbells would seem to be a Jacobite[47] rather than a Williamite[48] tradition. It may suggest interesting complications of Scottish feuds in Ireland; but it serves as one of a thousand cases of this fact about the family.

Let anybody imagine an Englishman saying about some business quarrel, "How like an Atkins!" or "What would you expect of a Wilkinson?" A moment's reflection will show that it would be even more impossible touching public men in public quarrels. No English Liberal ever connected the earlier exploits of the present Lord Birkenhead[49] with atavistic influences, or the totem of the wide and wandering tribe of Smith. No English patriot traced back the family tree of any English pacifist; or said there was never treason yet but a Pringle was at the bottom of it. It is the indefinite article that is here the definite distinction. It is the expression "a Campbell" which suddenly transforms the scene, and covers the robes of one lawyer with the ten thousand tartans of a whole clan. Now that phrase is the phrase that meets the traveller everywhere in Ireland. Perhaps the next most arresting thing I remember, after the agrarian revolution, was the way in which one poor Irishman happened to speak to me about Sir Roger Casement.[50] He did not praise him as a deliverer of Ireland; he did not say anything of the twenty things one might expect him to say. He merely referred to the rumour that Casement meant to become a Catholic just before his execution, and expressed a sort of distant interest in it. He added: "He's always been a Black Protestant. All the Casements are Black Protestants": I confess that, at that moment of that morbid story, there seemed to me to be something unearthly about the very idea of there being other Casements. If ever a man seemed solitary, if ever a man seemed unique to the point of being unnatural, it was that man on the two or three occasions when I have seen his sombre handsome face and his wild eye; a talk, dark figure walking already in the shadow of a dreadful doom. I do not know if he was a Black Protestant; but he was a black something, in the sad if not the bad sense of the symbol. I fancy, in truth, he stood rather for the third of Browning's[51] famous triad of rhyming monosyllables. A distinguished Nationalist Member, who happened to have had a medical training, said to me, "I was quite certain, when I first clapped eyes on him, the man was mad": Anyhow the man was so unusual, that it would never have occurred to me or any of my countrymen to talk as if there were a class or clan of such men. I could almost have imagined he had been born without father or mother. But for the Irish, his father and mother were really more important than he was. There is said to be a historical mystery about whether Parnell made a pun when he said that the name of Kettle[52] was a household word in Ireland. Few symbols could now be more contrary than the name of Kettle and the name of Casement (save for the courage they had in common); for the younger Kettle, who died so gloriously in France, was a Nationalist as broad as the other was cramped, and as sane as the other was crazy. But if the fancy of a punster, following his own delightful vein of nonsense, should see something quaint in the image of a hundred such Kettles singing as he sang by a hundred hearths, a more bitter jester, reading that black and obscure story of the capture on the coast, might utter a similar flippancy about other Casements, opening on the foam of such very perilous seas, in a land so truly forlorn. But even if we were not annoyed at the pun, we should be surprised at the plural. And our surprise would be the measure of the deepest difference between

England and Ireland. To express it in the same idle imagery, it would be the fact that even a casement is a part of a house, as a kettle is a part of a household. Every word in Irish is a household word. The English would no more have thought of a plural for the word Gladstone[53] than for the word God. They would never have imagined Disraeli[54] compassed about with a great cloud of Disraelis; it would have seemed to them altogether too apocalyptic an exaggeration of being on the side of the angels. To this day in England, as I have reason to know, it is regarded as a rabid and insane form of religious persecution to suggest that a Jew very probably comes of a Jewish family. In short, the modern English, while their rulers are willing to give due consideration to Eugenics as a reasonable opportunity for various forms of polygamy and infanticide, are drifting farther and farther from the only consideration of Eugenics that could possibly fit for Christian men, the consideration of it as an accomplished fact. I have spoken of infanticide; but indeed the ethic involved is rather that of parricide and matricide. To my own taste, the present tendency of social reform would seem to consist of destroying all traces of the parents, in order to study the heredity of the children. But I do not here ask the reader to accept my own tastes or even opinion about these things; I only bear witness to an objective fact about a foreign country. It can be summed up by saying that Parnell is the Parnell for the English; but a Parnell for the Irish.

This is what I mean when I say that the English Home Rulers do not know what the Irish mean by home. And this is also what I mean when I say that the society does not fit into any of our social classifications, liberal or conservative. To many Radicals this sense of lineage will appear rank reactionary aristocracy. And it is aristocratic, if we mean by this a pride of pedigree; but it is not aristocratic in the practical and political sense. Strange as it may sound, its practical effect is democratic. It is not aristocratic in the sense of creating an aristocracy. On the contrary, it is perhaps the one force that permanently prevents the creation of an aristocracy, in the manner of the English squirearchy. The reason of this apparent paradox can be put plainly enough in one sentence. If you are *really* concerned about your relations, you have to be concerned about your poor relations. You soon discover that a considerable number of your second cousins exhibit a strong social tendency to be chimney-sweepers and tinkers. You soon learn the lesson of human equality, if you try honestly and consistently to learn any other lesson, even the lesson of heraldry and genealogy. For good or evil, a real working aristocracy has to forget about three-quarters of its aristocrats. It has to discard the poor who have the genteel blood, and welcome the rich who can live the genteel life. If a man is interesting because he is a McCarthy, it is so far as he is interesting because he is a man; that is, he is interesting whether he is a duke or a dustman. But if he is interesting because he is Lord FitzArthur and lives at FitzArthur House, then he is interesting when he has merely bought the house, or when he has merely bought the title. To maintain a squirearchy it is necessary to admire the new squire, and therefore to forget the old squire. The sense of family is like a dog and follows the family; the sense of aristocracy is like a cat and continues to haunt the house. I am not arguing against aristocracy, if the English choose to preserve it in England; I am only making clear the terms on which they hold it, and warning them that a people with a strong family sense will not hold it on any terms. Aristocracy, as it has flourished in England since the Reformation, with not a little national glory and commercial success, is in its very nature built up of broken and desecrated homes. It has to destroy a hundred poor relations to keep up a family. It has to destroy a hundred families to keep up a class.

But if this family spirit is incompatible with what we mean by aristocracy, it is quite as incompatible with three-quarters of what many men praise and preach as democracy. The whole trend of what has been regarded as Liberal legislation in England, necessary or unnecessary, defensible and indefensible, has for good or evil been at the expense of the independence of the family, especially of the poor family. From the first most reasonable restraints of the Factory Acts[55] to the last most maniacal antics of interference with other people's nursery games or Christmas dinners, the whole process has turned sometimes on the pivot of the State, more often on the pivot of the employer, but never on the pivot of the home. All this may be emancipation; I only point out that Ireland really asked for Home

Rule chiefly to be emancipated from this emancipation. But indeed the English politicians, to do them justice, show their consciousness of this by the increasing number of cases in which the other nation is exempted. We may have harried this unhappy people with our persecutions; but at least we can spare them our reforms. We have smitten them with plagues; but at least we dare not scourge them with our remedies. The real case against the Union is not merely a case against the Unionists; it is a far stronger case against the Universalists. It is this strange and ironic truth; that a man stands up holding a charter of charity and peace for all mankind; that he lays down a law of enlightened justice for all the nations of the earth; that he claims to behold man from the beginning of his evolution equal, without any difference between the most distant creeds and colours; that he stands as the orator of the human race, whose statute only declares all humanity to be human; and slightly drops his voice and says, "This Act shall not apply to Ireland."

One scene of the incredible devastation at the center of Dublin, wrought by the massive British artillery bombardment during the 1916 Rebellion.

IV. The Paradox of Labour

Y FIRST GENERAL AND VISUAL IMPRESSION OF THE green island was that it was not green but brown; that it was positively brown with khaki. This is one of those experiences that cannot be confused with expectations; the sort of small thing that is seen but not foreseen in the verbal visions of books and newspapers. I knew, of course, that we had a garrison in Dublin, but I had no notion that it was so obvious all over Dublin. I had no notion that it had been considered necessary to occupy the country in such force, or with so much parade of force. And the first thought that flashed through my mind found words in the single sentence: "How useful these men would have been in the breach at St. Quentin."[56]

For I went to Dublin towards the end of 1918, and not long after those awful days which led up to the end of the war, and seemed more like the end of the world. There hung still in the imagination, as above a void of horror, that line that was the last chain of the world's chivalry; and the memory of the day when it seemed that our name and our greatness and our glory went down before the annihilation from the north. Ireland is hardly to blame if she has never known how noble an England was in peril in that hour; or for what beyond any empire we were troubled when, under a cloud of thick darkness, we almost felt her ancient foundations move upon the floor of the sea. But I, as an Englishman, at least knew it; and it was for England and not for Ireland that I felt this first impatience and tragic irony. I had always doubted the military policy that culminated in Irish conscription, and merely on military grounds. If any policy of the English could deserve to be called in the proverbial sense Irish, I think it was this one. It was wasting troops in Ireland because we wanted them in France. I had the same purely patriotic and even pugnacious sense of annoyance, mingling with my sense of pathos, in the sight of the devastation of the great Dublin street, which had been bombarded by the British troops during the Easter Rebellion. I was bitterly distressed that such a cannonade had ever been aimed at the Irish; but even more distressed that it had not been aimed at the Germans. The question of the necessity of the heavy attack, like the question of the necessity of the large army of occupation, is of course bound up with the history of the Easter Rebellion itself. That strange and dramatic event, which came quite as unexpectedly to Nationalist Ireland as to Unionist England, is no part of my own experiences, and I will not dogmatise on so dark a problem. But I will say, in passing, that I suspect a certain misunderstanding of its very nature to be common on both sides. Everything seems to point to the paradox that the rebels needed the less to be conquered, because they were actually aiming at being conquered, rather than at being conquerors. In the moral sense they were most certainly heroes, but I doubt if they expected to be conquering heroes. They desired to be in the Greek and literal sense martyrs; they wished not so much to win as to witness. They thought that nothing but their dead bodies could really prove that Ireland was not dead. How far this sublime and suicidal ideal was really useful in reviving national enthusiasm it is for Irishmen to judge; I should have said that the enthusiasm was there anyhow. But if any such action is based on international hopes, as they affect England or a great part of America, it seems to me founded on a fallacy about the facts. I shall have occasion to note many English errors about the Irish; and this seems to me a very notable Irish error about the English. If we are often utterly mistaken about their mentality, they were quite equally mistaken about our mistake. And curiously enough, they failed through not knowing the one compliment that we had always paid them. Their act presupposed that Irish courage needed proof; and it never did. I have heard all the most horrible nonsense talked against Ireland before the war; and I never heard Englishmen doubt Irish military valour. What they did doubt was Irish political sanity. It will be seen at once that the Easter action could only disprove the prejudice they hadn't got, and actually confirmed the prejudice they had got. The charge against the Irishman was not a lack of boldness, but rather an excess of it. Men were right in thinking him brave, and they could not be more right. But they were wrong in thinking him mad, and they had an excellent opportunity to be more wrong. Then, when the attempt to fight against England developed by its own logic into a refusal to fight for England, men took away the number they first thought of, and were irritated into denying what they had originally never dreamed of doubting. In any case, this was, I think, the temper in which the minority of the true Sinn Feiners sought martyrdom. I for one will never sneer at such a motive; but it would hardly have amounted to so great a movement but for another force that happened to ally itself to them. It is for the sake of this that I have here begun with the Easter tragedy itself; for with the consideration of this we come to the paradox of Irish Labour.

Some of my remarks on the stability and even repose of a peasant society may seem exaggerated in the light of a Labour agitation that breaks out in Ireland as elsewhere. But I have particular and even personal reasons for regarding that agitation as the exception that proves the rule. It was the background of the peasant landscape that made the Dublin strike the peculiar sort of drama that it was; and this operated in two ways; first, by isolating the industrial capitalist as something exceptional and almost fanatical; and second, by reinforcing the proletariat with a vague tradition of property. My own sympathies were all with Larkin[57] and Connolly[58] as against the late Mr. Murphy;[59] but it is curious to note that even Mr. Murphy was quite a different kind of man from the Lord Something who is the head of a commercial combine in England. He was much more like some morbid prince of the fifteenth century, full of cold anger, not without perverted piety. But the first few words I heard about him in Ireland were full of that vast, vague fact which I have tried to put first among my impressions. I have called it the family; but it covers many cognate things; youth and old friendships, not to mention old quarrels. It might be more fully defined as a realism about origins. The first things I heard about Murphy were facts of his forgotten youth, or a youth that would in England have been forgotten. They were tales about friends of his simpler days, with whom he had set out to push some more or less sentimental vendetta against somebody. Suppose whenever we talked of Harrod's Stores we heard first about the boyish day-dreams of Harrod. Suppose the mention of Bradshaw's Railway Guide brought up tales of feud and first love in the early life of Mr. Bradshaw, or even of Mrs. Bradshaw. That is the atmosphere, to be felt rather than described, that a stranger in Ireland feels around him. English journalism and gossip, dealing with English businessmen, are often precise about the present and prophetic about the future, but seldom communicative about the past; *et pour cause*.[60] They will tell us where the capitalist is going to, as to the House of Lords, or to Monte Carlo, or inferentially to heaven; but they say as little as possible about where he comes from. In Ireland a man carries the family mansion about with him like a snail; and his father's ghost follows him like his shadow. Everything good and bad that could be said was said, not only about Murphy but about Murphys. An anecdote of the old Irish Parliament describes an orator as gracefully alluding to the presence of an opponent's sister in the Ladies Gallery, by praying that wrath overtake the whole accursed generation "from the toothless hag who is grinning in the gallery to the white-livered poltroon who is shivering on the floor." The story is commonly told as suggesting the rather wild disunion of Irish parties; but it is quite as important a suggestion of the union of Irish families.

As a matter of fact, the great Dublin Strike, a conflagration of which the embers were still glowing at the time of my visit, involved another episode which illustrates once again this recurrent principle of the reality of the family in Ireland. Some English Socialists, it may be remembered, moved by an honourable pity for the poor families starving during the strike, made a proposal for taking the children away and feeding them properly in England. I should have thought the more natural course would have been to give money or food to the parents. But the philanthropists, being English and being Socialists, probably had a trust in what is called organization and a distrust of what is called charity. It is supposed that charity makes a man dependent; though in fact charity makes him independent, as compared with the dreary dependence usually produced by organization. Charity gives property, and therefore liberty. There is manifestly much more emancipation in giving a beggar a shilling to spend, than in sending an official after him to spend it for him. The Socialists, however, had placidly arranged for the deportation of all the poor children, when they found themselves, to their astonishment, confronted with the red-hot reality called the religion of Ireland. The priests and the families of the faithful organized themselves for a furious agitation, on the ground that the Faith would be lost in foreign and heretical homes. They were not satisfied with the assurance, which some of the Socialists earnestly offered, that the Faith would not be tampered with; and, as a matter of clear thinking, I think they were quite right. Those who offer such a reassurance have never thought about what a religion is. They entertain the extraordinary idea that religion is a topic. They think religion is a thing like radishes, which can be avoided throughout a particular conversation with a particular person, whom the mention of a radish may convulse with anger or agony. But a religion is simply the world a man inhabits. In practice, a Socialist living in Liverpool would not know when he was or was not tampering with the religion of a child born in Louth. If I were given the complete control of an infant Parsee[61] (which is fortunately unlikely) I should not have the remotest notion of when I was most vitally reflecting on the Parsee system. But common sense, and a comprehension of the meaning of a coherent philosophy, would lead me to suspect that I was reflecting on it every other minute. But I mention the matter here, not in order to enter into any of these disputes, but to give yet another example of the way in which the essentially domestic organization of Ireland will always rise in rebellion against any other organization. There is something of a parable in the tales of the old evictions, in which the whole family was besieged and resisted together and the mothers emptied boiling kettles on the besiegers; for any official who interferes with them will certainly get into hot water. We cannot separate mothers and children in that strange land. We can only return to some of our older historical methods and massacre them together.

A small incident within my own short experience, however, illustrated the main point involved here; the sense of a peasant base even of the proletarian attack. And this was exemplified not in any check to Labour, but rather in a success for Labour, insofar as the issue of a friendly and informal debate may be classed with its more solid successes. The business originally began with a sort of loose-jointed literary lecture which I gave in the Dublin Theatre, in connection with which I only mention two incidents in passing, because they both struck me as peculiarly native and national. One concerned only the title of my address, which was "Poetry and Property." An educated English gentleman, who happened to speak to me before the meeting, said with the air of one who foresees that such jokes will be the death of him, "Well, I have simply given up puzzling about what you can possibly mean, by talking about poetry as something to do with property." He probably regarded the combination of words as a mere alliterative fantasy, like Peacocks and Paddington, or Polygamy and Potatoes; if indeed he did not regard it as a mere combination of incompatible contrasts, like Popery and Protestants, or Patriotism and Politicians. On the same day an Irishman of similar social standing remarked quite carelessly, "I've just seen your subject for tomorrow. I suppose the Socialists will reply to you," or words to that effect. The two terms told him at once, not about the lecture (which was literary if it was anything), but about the whole philosophy underlying the lecture; the whole of that philosophy which the lumbering elephant called by Mr. Shaw the Chesterbelloc laboriously toils to explain in England, under the ponderous title of Distributism. As Mr. Hugh Law[62] once said, equally truly, about our pitting of patriotism against imperialism, "What is a paradox in England is a commonplace in Ireland." My actual monologue, however, dealt merely with the witness of poetry to a certain dignity in man's sense of private possession, which is certainly not either vulgar ostentation or vulgar greed. The French poet of the Pleiade remembers the slates on his own roof almost as if he could count them. And Mr. W.B. Yeats,[63] in the very wildest vision of a loneliness remote and irresponsible, is careful to make it clear that he knows how many bean-rows make nine. Of course there were people of all parties in the theatre, wild Sinn Feiners and conventional Unionists, but they all listened to my remarks as naturally as they might have all listened to an equally incompetent lecture on Monkeys or on the Mountains of the Moon. There was not a word of politics, least of all party politics, in that particular speech; it was concerned with a tradition in art, or at the most, in abstract ethics. But the one amusing thing which makes me recall the whole incident was this; that when I had finished a stalwart, hearty, heavy sort of legal gentleman, a well-know Irish judge I understand, was kind enough to move a vote of thanks to me. And what amused me about him was this: that while I (who am a Radical, in sympathy with the revolutionary legend) had delivered a mild essay on minor poets to a placid if bored audience, the judge, who was a pillar of the Castle and a Conservative sworn to law and order, proceeded with the utmost energy and joy to raise a riot. He taunted the Sinn Feiners and dared them to come out; he trailed his coat if ever a man trailed it in this world; he glorified England; not the Allies, but England; splendid England, sublime England (all in the broadest brogue), just, wise and merciful England, and so on, flourishing what was not even the flag of his own country, and a thing that had not the remotest connection with the subject in hand, any more than the Great Wall of China. I need not say that the theatre was soon in a roar of protests and repartees; which I suppose was what he wanted. He was a jolly old gentleman, and I liked him. But what interested me about him was this; and it is of some importance in the understanding of his nationality. That sort of man exists in England; I know and like scores of him. Often he is a major; often a squire; sometimes a judge; very occasionally a dean. Such a man talks the most ridiculous reactionary nonsense in an apoplectic fashion over his own port wine; and occasionally in a somewhat gasping manner at an avowedly political meeting. But precisely what the English gentleman would not do, and the Irish gentleman did do, would be to make a scene on a non-political occasion; when all he had to do was to move a formal vote of thanks to a total stranger, who was talking about Ithaca and Innisfree. An English Conservative would be less likely to do it than an English Radical. The same thing that makes him conventionally political would make him conventionally non-political. He would hate to make too serious a speech on too social an occasion, as he would hate to be in morning dress when everyone else was in evening dress. And whatever coat he wore he certainly would not trail it solely in order to make a disturbance, as did that jolly Irish judge. He taught me that the Irishman is never so Irish as when he is English. He was very like some of the Sinn Feiners who shouted him down; and he would be pleased to know that he helped me to understand them with a greater sympathy.

I have wandered from the subject in speaking of this trifle, thinking it worthwhile to note the positive and provocative quality of all Irish opinion; but it was my purpose only to mention this small dispute as leading up to another. I had some further talk about poetry and property with Mr. Yeats at the Dublin Arts Club; and here again I am tempted to irrelevant but for me interesting matters. For I am conscious throughout of saying less than I could wish of a thousand things, my omission of which is not altogether thoughtless, far less thankless. There have been and will be better sketches than mine of all that attractive society, the paradox of an intelligentsia that is intelligent. I could write a great deal, not only about those I value as my own friends, like Katherine Tynan[64] or Stephen Gwynn,[65] but about men with whom my meeting was all too momentary; about the elvish energy conveyed by Mr. James Stephens;[66] the social greatness of Dr. Gogarty,[67] who was like a witty legend of the eighteenth century; of the unique universalism of A.E., who has something of the presence of William Morris, and a more transcendental type of the spiritual hospitality of Walt Whitman.[68] But I am not in this rough sketch trying to tell Irishmen what they know already, but trying to tell Englishmen some of the large and simple things that they do not always know. The large matter concerned here is Labour; and I have only paused upon the other points because they were the steps which accidentally led up to my first meeting with this great force. And it was nonetheless a fact in support of my argument because it was something of a joke against myself.

On the occasion I have mentioned, a most exhilarating evening at the Arts Club, Mr. Yeats asked me to open a debate at the Abbey Theatre, defending property on its more purely political side. My opponent was one of the ablest of the leaders of Liberty Hall,[69] the famous stronghold of Labour politics in Dublin; Mr. Johnson,[70] an Englishman like myself, but one deservedly popular with the proletarian Irish. He made a most admirable speech, to which I mean no disparagement when I say that I think his personal popularity had even more weight than his personal eloquence. My own argument was confined to the particular value of small property as a weapon of militant democracy, and was based on the idea that the citizen resisting injustice could find no substitute for private property; for every other impersonal power, however democratic in theory, must be bureaucratic in form. I said, as a flippant figure of speech, that committing property to any officials, even guild officials, was like having to leave one's legs in the cloakroom along with one's stick or umbrella. The point is that a man may want his legs at any minute, to kick a man or to dance with a lady; and recovering them may be postponed by any hitch, from the loss of the ticket to the criminal flight of the official. So in a social crisis, such as a strike, a man must be ready to act without officials who may hamper or betray him; and I asked whether many more strikes would not have been successful, if each striker had owned so much as a kitchen garden to help him to live. My opponent replied that he had always been in favour of such a reserve of proletarian property, but preferred it to be communal rather than individual; which seems to me to leave the argument where it was; for what is communal must be official, unless it is to be chaotic. Two minor jokes, somewhat at my expense, remain in my memory. I appear to have caused some amusement by cutting a pencil with a very large Spanish knife, which I value (as it happens) as the gift of an Irish priest who is a friend of mine, and which may therefore also be regarded as a symbolic weapon, a sort of sword of the spirit. Whether the audience thought I was about to amputate my own legs in illustration of my own metaphor, or that I was going to cut Mr. Johnson's throat in fury at finding no reply to his arguments, I do not know. The other thing which struck me as funny was an excellent retort by Mr. Johnson himself, who had said something about the waste of property on guns, and who interrupted my remark that there would never be a good revolution without guns, by humorously calling out, "Treason." As I told him afterwards, few scenes would be more artistic than that of an Englishman, sent over to recruit for the British Army, being collared and given up to justice (or injustice) by a Pacifist from Liberty Hall. But all throughout the proceedings I was conscious, as I say, of a very real popular feeling supporting the mere personality of my opponent; as in the ovation he received before he spoke at all, or the applause given to a number of his topical asides, allusions which I could not always understand. After the meeting a distinguished Southern Unionist, who happens to own land outside Dublin, said to me, "Of course, Johnson has just had a huge success in his work here. Liberty Hall has just done something that has really never been done before in the whole Trade Union movement. He has really managed to start a Trade Union for agricultural labourers. I know, because I've had to meet their demands. You know how utterly impossible it has always really been to found a union of agricultural labourers in England." I did know it; and I also knew why it had been possible to found one in Ireland. It had been possible for the very reason I had been urging all the evening; that behind the Irish proletariat there had been the tradition of an Irish peasantry. In their families, if not in themselves, there had been some memory of the personal love of the land. But it seemed to me an interesting irony that even my own defeat was an example of my own doctrine; and that the truth on my side was proved by the popularity of the other side. The agricultural guild was due to a wind of freedom that came into that dark city from very distant fields; and the truth that even these rolling stones of homeless proletarianism had been so lately loosened from the very roots of the mountains.

In Ireland even the industrialism is not industrial. That is what I mean by saying that Irish Labour is the exception that proves the rule. That is why it does not contradict my former generalization that our capitalist crisis is on the English side of the road. The Irish agricultural labourers can become guildsmen because they would like to become peasants. They think of rich and poor in the manner that is as old as the world; the manner of Ahab and Naboth.[71] It matters little in a peasant society whether Ahab takes the vineyard privately as Ahab or officially as King of Israel. It will matter as little in the long run, even in the other kind of society, whether Naboth has a wage to work in the vineyard, or a vote that is supposed in some way to affect the vineyard. What he desires to have is the vineyard; and not in apologetic cynicism or vulgar evasions that business is business, but in thunder, as from a secret throne, comes the awful voice out of the vineyard; the voice of this manner of man in every age and nation: "The Lord forbid that I should give the inheritance of my fathers unto thee."

Above, Catholic women gathered outside Mountjoy Gaol, Dublin, in 1920.
The crescendo of violence between British forces and the IRA was rapidly approaching its peak, and many hundreds of Republican volunteers were imprisoned throughout the country. The combination of Prayer and Action was the hallmark of the struggle.
Irish women played a key role in most other aspects of the struggle against the British as well. Active in fund-raising, in organizing demonstrations, in saying the Rosary in public, in information-gathering, they were often the most committed of the Republican militants.
Below, another view of the gathering of women outside the gate at Mountjoy Gaol, ca. 1920, a gathering known to the British as "the Republican Scenic Railway."

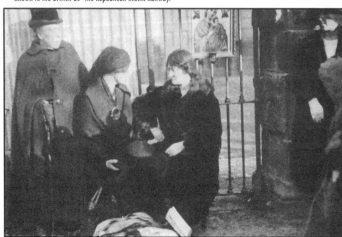

V. The Englishman in Ireland

ITH NO DESIRE TO DECORATE MY TRAVELS WITH too tall a traveller's tale, I must record the fact that I found one point upon which all Irishmen were agreed. It was the fact that, for some reason or other, there had been a very hopeful beginning of Irish volunteering at the beginning of the war; and that, for some reason or other, this had failed in the course of the war. The reasons alleged differed widely with the moods of men; some had regarded the beginning with hope and some with suspicion; some had lived to regard the failure with a bitter pleasure, and some with a generous pain. The different factions gave different explanations of why the thing had stopped; but they all agreed that it had begun. The Sinn Feiner said that the people soon found they had been lured into a Saxon trap, set for them by smooth subservient Saxons like Mr. Devlin[72] and Mr. Tim Healy.[73] The Belfast citizen suggested that the Popish priest had terrorized the peasants when they tried to enlist, producing a thumbscrew from his pocket and a portable rack from his handbag. The Parliamentary Nationalist blamed both Sinn Fein and the persecution of Sinn Fein. The British Government officials, if they did not exactly blame themselves, at least blamed each other. The ordinary Southern Unionist (who played many parts of a more or less sensible sort, including that of a Home Ruler) generally agreed with the ordinary Nationalist that the Government's recruiting methods had been as bad as its cause was good. But it is manifest that multitudes at the beginning of the war thought it really had a very good cause; and, moreover, a very good chance.

The extraordinary story of how that chance was lost may find mention on a later page. I will begin by touching on the first incident that befell me personally in connection with the same enterprise. I went to Ireland at the request of Irish friends who were working warmly for the Allied cause, and who conceived (I fear in far too flattering a spirit) that I might at least be useful as an Englishman who had always sympathized warmly with the Irish cause. I am under no illusions that I should ever be efficient at such work in any case; and under the circumstances I had no great hopes of doing much, where men like Sir Horace Plunkett and Captain Stephen Gwynn, far more competent, more self-sacrificing, and more well-informed than I, could already do comparatively little. It was too late. A hundredth part of the brilliant constancy and tragic labours of these men might easily, at the beginning of the war, have given us a great Irish army. I need not explain the motives that made me do the little I could do; they were the same that at that moment made millions of better men do masses of better work. Physical accident prevented my being useful in France, and a sort of psychological accident seemed to suggest that I might possibly be useful in Ireland; but I did not see myself as a very serious figure in either field. Nothing could be serious in such a case except perhaps a conviction; and at least my conviction about the Great War has never wavered by a hair. *Delenda est*[74] – and it is typical of the power of Berlin that one must break off for want of a Latin name for it. Being an Englishman, I hoped primarily to help England; but not being a congenital idiot, I did not primarily ask an Irishman to help England. There was obviously something much more reasonable to ask him to do. I hope I should in any case have done my best for my own country. But the cause was more than any country; in a sense it was too good for any country. The Allies were more right than they realized. Nay, they hardly had a right to be so right as they were. The modern Babylon of capitalistic States was hardly worthy to go on such a crusade against the heathen; as perhaps decadent Byzantium[75] was hardly worthy to defend the Cross against the Crescent.[76] But we are glad that it did defend the Cross against the Crescent. Nobody is sorry that Sobieski[77] relieved Vienna; nobody wishes that Alfred had not won in Wessex.[78] The cause that conquered is the only cause that survived. We see now that its enemy was not a cause but a chaos; and that is what history will say

The Englishman in Ireland 65

of the strange and recent boiling up of barbaric imperialism, a whirlpool whose hollow centre was Berlin. This is where the extreme Irish were really wrong; perhaps really wrong for the first time. I entirely sympathize with their being in revolt against the British Government. I am in revolt in most ways against the British Government myself. But politics are a fugitive thing in the face of history. Does anybody want to be fixed forever on the wrong side at the Battle of Marathon, through a quarrel with some Archon whose very name is forgotten?[79] Does anybody want to be remembered as a friend of Attila, through a breach of friendship with Ætius?[80] In any case, it was with a profound conviction that if Prussia won Europe must perish, and that if Europe perished England and Ireland must perish together, that I went to Dublin in those dark days of the last year of the war; and it so happened that the first occasion when I was called upon for any expression of opinion was at a very pleasant luncheon party given to the representatives of the British Dominions, who were then on an official tour in the country inspecting its conditions. What I said is of no importance except as leading up to later events; but it may be noted that though I was speaking perhaps indirectly to Irishmen, I was speaking directly, if not to Englishmen, at least to men in the more English tradition of the majority of the Colonies. I was speaking, if not to Unionists, at least largely to Imperialists.

Now I have forgotten, I am happy to say, the particular speech that I made, but I can repeat the upshot of it here, not only as part of the argument, but as part of the story. The line I took generally in Ireland was an appeal to the Irish principle, yet the reverse of a mere approval of the Irish action, or inaction. It postulated that while the English had missed a great opportunity of justifying themselves to the Irish, the Irish had also missed a similar opportunity of justifying themselves to the English. But it specially emphasized this; that what had been lost was not primarily a justification against England, but a joke against England. I pointed out that an Irishman missing a joke against an Englishman was a tragedy, like a lost battle. And there was one thing, and one thing only, which had stopped the Irishman from laughing and saved the Englishman from being laughable. The one and only thing that rescued England from ridicule was Sinn Fein. Or, at any rate, that element in Sinn Fein which was pro-German, or refused to be anti-German. Nothing imaginable under the stars *except* a pro-German Irishman could at that moment have saved the face of a (very recently) pro-German Englishman.

The reason for this is obvious enough. England in 1914 encountered or discovered a colossal crime of Prussianized Germany. But England could not discover the German crime without discovering the English blunder. The blunder was, of course, a perfectly plain historical fact; that England made Prussia. England was the historic, highly civilized western state, with Roman foundations and chivalric memories; Prussia was originally a petty and boorish principality used by England and Austria in the long struggle against the greatness of France. Now in that long struggle Ireland had always been on the side of France. She had only to go on being on the side of France, and the Latin tradition generally, to behold her own truth triumph over her own enemies. In a word, it was not a question of whether Ireland should become anti-German, but merely of whether she should *continue* to be anti-German. It was a question of whether she should suddenly become pro-German, at the moment when most other pro-Germans were discovering that she had been justified all along. But England, at the beginning of her last and most lamentable quarrel with Ireland, was by no means in so strong a controversial position. England was right; but she could only prove she was right by proving she was wrong. In one sense, and with all respect to her right action in the matter, she had to be ridiculous in order to be right.

But the joke against the English was even more obvious and topical. And as mine was only meant for a light speech after a friendly lunch, I took the joke in its lightest and most fanciful form, and touched chiefly on the fantastic theory of the Teuton as the master of the Celt. For the supreme joke was this: that the Englishman has not only boasted of being an Englishman; but he has actually boasted of being a German. As the modern mind began to doubt the superiority of Calvinism to Catholicism, all English books, papers and speeches were filled more and more with a Teutonism which substituted a racial for a religious superiority. It was felt to be a more modern and even more progressive principle of distinction, to insist on ethnology rather than theology: for ethnology was supposed to be a science. Unionism was simply founded on Teutonism. Hence the ordinary honest patriotic Unionist was in a highly humorous fix when he had suddenly to begin denouncing Teutonism as mere terrorism. If all superiority belonged to the Teuton, the supreme superiority must clearly belong to the most Teutonic Teuton. If I claim the right to kick Mr. Bernard Shaw on the specific ground that I am fatter than he is, it is obvious that I look rather a fool if I am suddenly kicked by something who is fatter still. When the earth shakes under the advancing form of one coming against me out of the east who is fatter than I (for I called upon the Irish imagination to embrace so monstrous a vision), it is clear that whatever my relations to the rest of the world, in my relations to Mr. Bernard Shaw I am rather at a disadvantage. Mr. Shaw, at any rate, is rather in a position to make game of me; of which it is not inconceivable that he might avail himself. I might have accumulated a vast mass of learned sophistries and journalistic catchwords, which had always seemed to me to justify the connection between waxing fat and kicking. I might have proved from history that the leaders had always been fat men, like William the Conqueror,[81] St. Thomas Aquinas[82] and Charles Fox.[83] I might have proved from physiology that fatness is a proof of the power of organic assimilation and digestion; or from comparative zoology that the elephant is the wisest of the beasts. In short, I might be able to adduce many arguments in favour of my position. Only, unfortunately, they would now all become arguments against my position. Everything I had ever urged against my old enemy could be urged much more forcibly against me by my new enemy. And my position touching the great adipose theory would be exactly like England's position touching the equally sensible Teutonic theory. If Teutonism was creative culture, then on our own showing the German was better than the Englishman. If Teutonism was barbarism, then on our own showing the Englishman was more barbaric than the Irishman. The real answer, of course, is that we were not Teutons but only the dupes of Teutonism; but some were so wholly duped that they would do anything rather than own themselves duped. These unfortunates, while they are already ashamed of being Teutons, are still proud of not being Celts.

There is only one thing that could save my dignity in such an undignified fix as I have fancied here. It is that Mr. Bernard Shaw himself should come to my rescue. It is that Mr. Bernard Shaw himself should declare in favour of the corpulent conqueror from the east; that *he* should take seriously all the fads and fancies of that fat-headed superman. That, and that alone, would ensure all my own fads and fallacies being not only forgotten, but forgiven. There is present to my imagination, I regret to say, a wild possibility that this is what Mr. Bernard Shaw might really do. Anyhow, this is what a certain number of his countrymen really did. It will be apparent, I think, from these pages that I do not believe in the stage Irishman. I am under no delusion that the Irishman is soft-headed and sentimental, or even illogical and inconsequent. Nine times out of ten the Irishman is not only more clear-headed, but even more cool-headed than the Englishman. But I think it is true, as Mr. Max Beerbohm[84] once suggested to me in connection with Mr. Shaw himself, that there is a residual perversity in the Irishman, which comes after and not before the analysis of a question. There is at the last moment a cold impatience in the intellect, an irony which returns on itself and rends itself; the subtlety of a suicide. However this may be, some of the lean men, instead of making a fool of the fat man, did begin almost to make a hero of the fatter man; to admire his vast curves as almost cosmic lines of development. I have seen Irish-American pamphlets which took quite seriously (or, I prefer to think, pretended to take quite seriously) the ridiculous romance about the Teutonic tribes having revived and refreshed civilization after the fall of the Roman Empire. They revived civilization very much as they restored Louvain or reconstructed the *Lusitania*.[85] It was a romance which the English for a short time adopted as a convenience, but from which the Irish have continually suffered as from a curse. It was a suicidal perversity that they themselves, in their turn, should perpetuate their permanent curse as a temporary convenience. That was the worst error of the Irish, or of some of the best of the Irish. That is why the Easter Rising was really a black and insane blunder. It was not because it involved the Irish in a military defeat; it was because it lost the Irish a great controversial victory. The rebel deliberately let the tyrant out of a trap; out of the grinning jaws of the gigantic trap of a joke. Many of the most extreme Nationalists knew this well; it was what Kettle probably meant when he suggested an Anglo-Irish history called "The Two Fools"; and of course I do not mean that I said all this in my very casual and rambling speech. But it was based on this idea, that men had missed the joke against England, and that now unfortunately the joke was rather against Ireland. It was Ireland that was now missing a great historical opportunity for lack of humour and imagination, as England had missed it a moment before. If the Irish would laugh at the English and help the English, they would win all along the line. In the real history of the German problem, they would inherit all the advantages of having been right from the first. It was now not so much a question of Ireland consenting to follow England's lead as of England being obliged to follow Ireland's lead. These are the principles which I thought, and still think, the only possible principles to form the basis of a recruiting appeal in Ireland. But on the particular occasion in question I naturally took the matter much more lightly, hoping that the two jokes might, as it were, cancel out and leave the two countries quits and in a better humour. And I devoted nearly all my remarks to testifying that the English had really, in the mass, shed the cruder Teutonism that had excused the cruelties of the past. I said that Englishmen were anything but proud of the past government of Ireland; that the mass of men of all parties were far more modest and humane in their view of Ireland than most Irishmen seem to suppose. And I ended with words which I only quote here from memory, because they happen to be the text of the curious incident which followed: "This is no place for us to boast. We stand here in the valley of our humiliation, where the flag we love has done very little that was not evil, and where its victories have been far more disastrous than defeats." And I concluded with some general expression of the hope (which I still entertain) that two lands so much loved, by those who know them best, are not meant to hate each other forever.

A day or two afterwards a distinguished historian who is a Professor at Trinity College, Mr. Alison Phillips,[86] wrote an indignant letter to the *Irish Times*. He announced that he was not in the valley of humiliation, and warmly contradicted the report that he was, as he expressed it, "sitting in sackcloth and ashes." He remarked, if I remember right, that I was middle-class, which is profoundly true; and he generally resented my suggestions as a shameful attack upon my fellow Englishmen. This both amused and puzzled me; for of course I had not been attacking Englishmen, but defending them; I had merely been assuring the Irish that the English were not so black, or so red, as they were painted in the vision of "England's cruel red." I had not said there what I have said here, about the anomaly and absurdity of England in Ireland; I had only said that Ireland had suffered rather from the Teutonic theory than the English temper; and that the English temper, experienced at close quarters, was really quite ready for a reconciliation with Ireland. Nor indeed did Mr. Alison Phillips really complain especially of my denouncing the English, but rather of my way of defending them. He did not so much mind being charged with the vice of arrogance. What he could not bear was being charged with the virtue of humility. What worried him was not so much the supposition of our doing wrong, as that anybody should conceive it possible that we were sorry for doing wrong. After all, he probably reasoned, it may not be easy for an eminent historical scholar actually to deny that certain tortures have taken place, or certain perjuries been proved; but there is really no reason why he should admit that the memory of using torture or perjury has so morbid an effect on the mind. Therefore he naturally desired to correct any impression that might arise, to the effect that he had been seen in the valley of humiliation, like a man called Christian.

But there was one fancy that lingered in the mind over and above the fun of the thing; and threw a sort of random ray of conjecture upon all that long international misunderstanding which it is so hard to understand. Was it possible, I thought, that this had happened before, and that I was caught in the treadmill of recurrence? It may be whenever, throughout the centuries, a roughly representative and fairly good-humoured Englishman has spoken to the Irish as thousands of such Englishman feel about them, some other Englishman on the spot has hastened to explain that the English are not going in for sackcloth and ashes, but only for phylacteries and the blowing of their own trumpets before them. Perhaps whenever one Englishman said that the English were not so black as they were painted in the past, another Englishman always rushed forward to prove that the English were not so white as they were painted on the present occasion. And after all it was only Englishman against Englishman, one word against another; and there were many superiorities on the side which refused to believe in English sympathy or self-criticism. And very few of the Irish, I fear, understood the simple fact of the matter, or the real spiritual excuses of the party thus praising spiritual pride. Few understood that I represented large numbers of amiable Englishmen in England, while Mr. Phillips necessarily represented a small number of naturally irritable Englishmen in Ireland. Few, I fancy, sympathized with him so much as I do; for I know very well that he was not merely feeling as an Englishman, but as an exile.

The defeated Volunteers of the 1916 Rebellion being led through the streets of Dublin. Loathed, spat upon, and reviled by much of the Dublin populace, they were to become the heroes of the Irish people within a year or so.

VI. The Mistake of England

I MET ONE HEARTY UNIONIST, NOT TO SAY COERcionist in Ireland, in such a manner as to talk to him at some length; one quite genial and genuine Irish gentleman, who was solidly on the side of the system of British Government in Ireland. This gentleman had been shot through the body by the British troops in their efforts to suppress the Easter Rebellion. The matter just missed being tragic; but since it did, I cannot help feeling it as slightly comic. He assured me with great earnestness that the rebels had been guilty of the most calculated cruelties, and that they must have done their bloody deeds in the coldest blood. But since he is himself a solid and (I am happy to say) a living demonstration that the firing even on his own side must have been rather wild, I am inclined to give the benefit of the doubt also to the less elaborately educated marksmen. When disciplined troops destroy people so much at random, it would seem unreasonable to deny that rioters may possibly have been riotous. I hardly think he was, or even professed to be, a person of judicial impartiality; and it is entirely to his honour that he was, on principle, so much more indignant with the rioters who did not shoot him than with the other rioters who did. But I venture to introduce him here not so much as an individual as an allegory. The incident seems to me to set forth, in a pointed, lucid and picturesque form, exactly what the British military government really succeeded in doing in Ireland. It succeeded in half-killing its friends, and affording an intelligent but somewhat inhumane amusement to all its enemies. The fire-eater held his fire-arm in so contorted a posture as to give the wondering spectator a simple impression of suicide.

The Mistake of England

Let it be understood that I speak here, not of tyranny thwarting Irish desires, but solely of our own stupidity in thwarting our own desires. I shall discuss elsewhere the alleged presence or absence of practical oppression in Ireland; here I am only continuing from the last chapter my experiences of the recruiting campaign. I am concerned now, as I was concerned then, with the simple business matter of getting a big levy of soldiers from Ireland. I think it was Sir Francis Vane, one of the few really valuable public servants in the matter (I need not say he was dismissed for having been proved right) who said that the mere sight of some representative Belgian priests and nuns might have produced something like a crusade. The matter seems to have been mostly left to elderly English landlords; and it would be cruel to record their adventures. It will be enough that I heard, on excellent testimony, that these unhappy gentlemen had displayed throughout Ireland a poster consisting only of the Union Jack and the appeal, "Is not this your flag? Come and fight for it!" It faintly recalls something we all learnt in the Latin grammar about questions that expect the answer no. These remarkable recruiting sergeants did not realize, I suppose, what an extraordinary thing this was, not merely in Irish opinion, but generally in international opinion. Over a great part of the globe, it would sound like a story that the Turks had placarded Armenia[87] with the Crescent of Islam, and asked all the Christians who were not yet massacred whether they did not love the flag. I really do not believe that the Turks would be so stupid as to do it. Of course it may be said that such an impression or association is mere slander and sedition, that there is no reason to be tender to such treasonable emotions at all, that men ought to do their duty to that flag whatever is put upon that poster; in short, that it is the duty of an Irishman to be a patriotic Englishman, or whatever it is that he is expected to be. But this view, however logical and clear, can only be used logically and clearly as an argument for conscription. It is simply muddle-headed to apply it to any appeal for volunteers anywhere, in Ireland or England. The whole object of a recruiting poster, or any poster, is to be attractive; it is picked out in words or colours to be picturesquely and pointedly attractive. If it lowers you to make an attractive offer, do not make it; but do not deliberately make it, and deliberately make it repulsive. If a certain medicine is so mortally necessary and so mortally nasty, that it must be forced on everybody by the policeman, call the policeman. But do not call an advertisement agent to push it like a patent medicine, solely by means of "publicity" and "suggestion," and then confine him strictly to telling the public how nasty it is.

But the British blunder in Ireland was a much deeper and more destructive thing. It can be summed up in one sentence; that whether or no we were as black as we were painted, we actually painted ourselves much blacker than we were. Bad as we were, we managed to look much worse than we were. In a horrible unconsciousness we re-enacted history through sheer ignorance of history. We were foolish enough to dress up, and to play up, to the part of a villain in a very old tragedy. We clothed ourselves almost carelessly in fire and sword; and if the fire had been literally stage-fire or the sword a wooden sword, the merely artistic blunder would have been quite as bad. For instance, I soon came on the traces of a quarrel about some silly veto in the schools, against Irish children wearing green rosettes. Anybody with a streak of historical imagination would have avoided a quarrel in that particular case about that particular colour. It is touching the talisman, it is naming the name, it is striking the note of another relation in which we were in the wrong, to the confusion of a new relation in which we were in the right. Anybody of common sense, considering any other case, can see the almost magic force of these material coincidences. If the English armies in France in 1914 considered themselves justified for some reason in executing some French woman, they would perhaps be indiscreet if they killed her (however logically) tied to a stake in the market place of Rouen. If the people of Paris rose in the most righteous revolt against the most corrupt conspiracy of some group of wealthy French Protestants, I should strongly advise them not to fix the date for the vigil of St. Bartholomew, or to go to work with white scarves tied around their arms. Many of us hope to see a Jewish commonwealth reconstituted in Palestine; and we could easily imagine some quarrel in which the government of Jerusalem was impelled to punish some Greek or Latin pilgrim or monk. The

Jews might even be right in the quarrel and the Christian wrong. But it may be hinted that the Jews would be ill-advised if they actually crowned him with thorns, and killed him on a hill just outside Jerusalem. Now we must know by this time, or the sooner we know it the better, that the whole mind of that European society which we have helped to save, and in which we have henceforth a part right of control, regards the Anglo-Irish story as one of those black and white stories in a history book. It sees the tragedy of Ireland as simply and clearly as the tragedy of Christ or Joan of Arc. There may have been more to be said on the coercive side than the culture of the Continent understands. So there was a great deal more than is usually admitted to be said on the side of the patriotic democracy which condemned Socrates; and a very great deal to be said on the side of the imperial aristocracy which would have crushed Washington. But these disputes will not take Socrates from his niche among the pagan saints, or Washington from his pedestal among the republican heroes. After a certain testing time substantial justice is always done to the men who stood in some unmistakable manner for liberty and light against contemporary caprice and fashionable force and brutality. In this intellectual sense, in the only competent intellectual courts, there is already justice to Ireland. In the wide daylight of this worldwide fact we or our representatives must get into a quarrel with children, of all people, and about the colour green, of all things in the world. It is an exact working model of the mistake I mean. It is the more brutal because it is not strictly cruel; and yet instantly revives the memories of cruelty. There need be nothing wrong with it in the abstract, or in a less tragic atmosphere where the symbols were not talismans. A schoolmaster in the prosperous and enlightened town of Eatanswill might not unpardonably protest against the school children parading in class in Buff and Blue in favour of Mr. Fizkin and Mr. Slumkey.[88] But who but a madman would not see that to say that word, or make that sign, in Ireland, was like giving a signal for keening and the lament over lost justice that is lifted in the burden of the noblest of national songs; that to point to that rag of that colour was to bring back all the responsibilities and realities of that reign of terror when we were, quite literally, hanging men and women too for wearing of the green? We were not literally hanging these children. As a matter of mere utility, we should have been more sensible if we had been.

But the same fact took an even more fantastic form. We not only dressed up as our ancestors, but we actually dressed up as our enemies. I need hardly state my own conviction that the Pacifist trick of lumping the abuses of one side along with the abominations of the other was a shallow pedantry come of sheer ignorance of the history of Europe and the barbarians. It was quite false that the English evil was exactly the same as the German. It was quite false; but the English in Ireland laboured long and devotedly to prove it was quite true. They were not content with borrowing old uniforms from the Hessians of 1789; they borrowed the newest and neatest uniforms from the Prussians of 1914. I will give only one story that I was told, out of many, to show what I mean. There was a sort of village musical festival at a place called Cullen in County Cork, at which there were naturally national songs and very possibly national speeches. That there was a sort of social atmosphere, which its critics would call Sinn Fein, is exceedingly likely; for that now exists all over Ireland, and especially that part of Ireland. If we wish to prevent it being expressed at all, we must not only forbid all public meetings but all private meetings, and even the meeting of husband and wife in their own house. Still there might have been a case, on coercionist lines, for forbidding this public meeting, for imprisoning all the people who attended it; or a still clearer case, on those lines, for imprisoning all the people in Ireland. But the coercionist authorities did not merely forbid the meeting, which would mean something. They did not arrest the people at the meeting, which would mean something. They did not blow the whole meeting to hell with big guns, which would also mean something. What they did apparently was this. They caused a military aeroplane to jerk itself backwards and forwards in a staggering fashion just over the heads of the people, making as much noise as possible to drown the music, and dropping flare rockets and fire in various somewhat dangerous forms in the neighbourhood of any men, women and children who happened to be listening to the music. The reader will note with what exquisite art, and fine fastidious selection, the strategist has here contrived to look

The Mistake of England

as Prussian as possible without securing any of the advantages of Prussianism. I do not know exactly how much danger there was, but there must have been some. Perhaps about as much as there generally has been when boys have been flogged for playing the fool with fireworks. But by laboriously climbing hundreds of feet into the air, in an enormous military machine, these ingenuous people managed to make themselves a meteor in heaven and a spectacle to all the earth; the English raining fire on women and children just as the Germans did. I repeat that they did not actually destroy children, though they did endanger them; for playing with fireworks is always playing with fire. And I repeat that, as a mere matter of business, it would have been more sensible if they had destroyed children. That would at least have had the human meaning that has run through a hundred massacres: "wolf cubs who would grow into wolves." It might at least have the execrable excuse of decreasing the number of rebels. What they did would quite certainly increase it.

An artless Member of Parliament, whose name I forget, attempted an apology for this half-witted performance. He interposed in the Unionist interest, when the Nationalists were asking questions about the matter, and said with much heat, "May I ask whether honest and loyal subjects have anything to fear from British aeroplanes?" I have often wondered what he meant. It seems possible that he was in the mood of that medieval fanatic who cried, "God will know His own";[89] and that he himself would fling any sort of flaming bolts about anywhere, believing that they would always be miraculously directed towards the heads harbouring, at that moment, the most incorrect political opinions. Or perhaps he meant that loyal subjects are so superbly loyal that they do not mind being accidentally burnt alive, so long as they are assured that the fire was dropped on them by Government officials out of a Government apparatus. But my purpose here is not to fathom such a mystery, but merely to fix the dominant fact of the whole situation; that the Government copied the theatricality of Potsdam even more than the tyranny of Potsdam. In that incident the English laboriously reproduced all the artificial accessories of the most notorious crimes of Germany; the flying men, the flame, the selection of a mixed crowd, the selection of a popular festival. They had every part of it, except the point of it. It was as if the whole British Army in Ireland had dressed up in spiked helmets and spectacles, merely that they might *look* like Prussians. It was even more as if a man had walked across Ireland on three gigantic stilts, taller than the trees and visible from the most distant village, solely that he might look like one of those unhuman monsters from Mars, striding about on their iron tripods in the great nightmare of Mr. Wells. Such was our educational efficiency that, before the end, multitudes of simple Irish people really had about the English invasion the same particular psychological reaction that multitudes of simple English people had about the German invasion. I mean that it seemed to come not only from outside the nation, but from outside the world. It was unearthly in the strict sense in which a comet is unearthly. It was the more appallingly alien for coming close; it was the more outlandish the farther it went inland. These Christian peasants have seen coming westward out of England what we saw coming westward out of Germany. They saw science in arms; which turns the very heavens into hells.

I have purposely put these fragmentary and secondary impressions before any general survey of Anglo-Irish policy in the war. I do so, first because I think a record of the real things, that seemed to bulk biggest to any real observer at any real moment, is often more useful than the setting forth of theories he may have made up before he saw any realities at all. But I do it in the second place because the more general summaries of our statesmanship, or lack of statesmanship, are so much more likely to be found elsewhere. But if we wish to comprehend the queer cross-purposes, it will be well to keep always in mind a historical fact I have mentioned already; the reality of the old Franco-Irish Entente. It lingers alive in Ireland, and especially the most Irish parts of Ireland. In the fiercely Fenian city of Cork, walking around the Young Ireland monument that seems to give revolt the majesty of an institution, a man told me that German bands had been hooted and pelted in those streets out of an indignant memory of 1870. And an eminent scholar in the same town, referring to the events of the same "terrible year," said to me: "In 1870 Ireland sympathized with France and England with Germany; and, as usual,

The Mistake of England

Ireland was right!" But if they were right when we were wrong, they only began to be wrong when we were right. A sort of play or parable might be written to show that this apparent paradox is a very genuine piece of human psychology. Suppose there are two partners named John and James; that James had always been urging the establishment of a branch of the business in Paris. Long ago John quarrelled with this furiously as a foreign fad; but he has since forgotten all about it; for the letters from James bored him so much that he has not opened any of them for years. One fine day John, finding himself in Paris, conceives the original idea of a Paris branch; but he is conscious in a confused way of having quarrelled with his partner, and vaguely feels that his partner would be an obstacle to anything. John remembers that James was always cantankerous, and forgets that he was cantankerous in favour of this project, and not against it. John therefore sends James a telegram, of a brevity amounting to brutality, simply telling him to come in with no nonsense about it; and when he has no instant reply, sends a solicitor's letter to be followed by a writ. How James will take it depends very much on James. How he will hail this happy confirmation of his own early opinions will depend on whether James is an unusually patient and charitable person. And James is not. He is unfortunately the very man, of all men in the world, to drop his original agreement and everything else into the black abyss of disdain, which now divides him from the man who has the impudence to agree with him. He is the very man to say he will have nothing to do with his own original notion, because it is now the belated notion of a fool. Such a character could easily be analysed in any good novel. Such conduct would readily be believed in any good play. It could not be believed when it happened in real life. And it did happen in real life; the Paris project was the sense of the safety of Paris as the pivot of human history; the abrupt telegram was the recruiting campaign, and the writ was conscription.

As to what Irish conscription was, or rather would have been, I cannot understand any visitor in Ireland having the faintest doubt, unless (as is often the case) his tour was so carefully planned as to permit him to visit everything in Ireland except the Irish. Irish conscription was a piece of rank raving madness, which was fortunately stopped, with other bad things, by the blow of Foch at the second battle of the Marne.[90] It could not possibly produce at the last moment allies on whom we could depend; and it would have lost us the whole sympathy of the allies on whom we at that moment depended. I do not mean that American soldiers would have mutinied; though Irish soldiers might have done so; I mean something much worse. I mean that the whole mood of America would have altered; and there would have been some kind of compromise with German tyranny, in sheer disgust at a long exhibition of English tyranny. Things would have happened in Ireland, week after week, and month after month, such as the modern imagination has not seen except where Prussia has established hell. We should have butchered women and children; they would have *made us* butcher them. We should have killed priests, and probably the best priests. It could not be better stated than in the words of an Irishman, as he stood with me in a high terraced garden outside Dublin, looking towards that unhappy city, who shook his head and said sadly, "They will shoot the wrong bishop."

Of the meaning of this huge furnace of defiance I shall write when I write of the national idea itself. I am concerned here not for their nation but for mine; and especially for its peril from Prussia and its help from America. And it is simply a question of considering what these real things are really like. Remember that the American Republic is practically founded on the fact, or fancy, that England is a tyrant. Remember that it was being ceaselessly swept with new waves of immigrant Irishry telling tales (too many of them true, though not all) of the particular cases in which England had been a tyrant. It would be hard to find a parallel to explain to Englishmen the effect of awakening traditions so truly American by a prolonged display of England as the tyrant of Ireland. A faint approximation might be found if we imagined the survivors of Victorian England, steeped in the tradition of *Uncle Tom's Cabin*, watching the American troops march through London. Suppose they noted that the negro troops alone had to march in chains, with a white man in a broad-brimmed hat walking beside them and flourishing a whip. Scenes far worse than that would have followed Irish conscription; but the only purpose of this chapter is to show that scenes quite as stupid marked every stage of Irish recruitment. For it certainly would not have reassured the traditional sympathizers with Uncle Tom to be told that the chains were only a part of the uniform, or that the niggers moved not at the touch of the whip, but only at the crack of it.

Such was our practical policy; and the single and sufficient comment on it can be found in a horrible whisper which can scarcely now be stilled. It is said, with a dreadful plausibility, that the Unionists were deliberately trying to prevent a large Irish recruitment, which would certainly have meant reconciliation and reform. In plain words, it is said that they were willing to be traitors to England, if they could only still be tyrants in Ireland. Only too many facts can be made to fit in with this; but for me it is still too hideous to be easily believed. But whatever our motives in doing it, there is simply no doubt whatever about what we did, in this matter of the Pro-Germans in Ireland. We did not crush the Pro-Germans; we did not convert them, or coerce them, or educate them or exterminate them or massacre them. We manufactured them; we turned them out patiently, steadily and systematically as if from a factory; we made them exactly as we made munitions. It needed no little social science to produce, in any kind of Irishman, any kind of sympathy with Prussia; but we were equal to the task. What concerns me here, however, is that we were busy at the same work among the Irish-Americans, and ultimately among all the Americans. And that would have meant, as I have already noted, the thing that I always feared; the dilution of the policy of the Allies. Anything that looked like a prolonged Prussianism in Ireland would have meant a compromise; that is, a perpetuated Prussianism in Europe. I know that some who agree with me in other matters disagree with me in this; but I should indeed be ashamed if, having to say so often where I think my country was wrong, I did not say as plainly where I think she was right. The notion of a compromise was founded on the coincidence of recent national wars, which were only about the terms of peace, not about the type of civilization. But there do recur, at longer historical intervals, universal wars of religion, not concerned with what one nation shall do, but with what all nations shall be. They recommence until they are finished, in things like the fall of Carthage or the rout of Attila. It is quite true that history is for the most part a plain road, which the tribes of men must travel side by side, bargaining at the same markets or worshipping at the same shrines, fighting and making friends again; and wisely making friends quickly. But we need only see the road stretch but a little farther, from a hill but a little higher, to see that sooner or later the road comes always to another place, where stands a winged image of victory; and the ways divide.

Troops, tanks and armored cars guarding the entrance to Mountjoy Gaol in Dublin, in April, 1920.

Inside the prison, some 80 Irish Republicans were on hunger strike, demanding to be recognized as political prisoners and not listed as common criminals. Whatever doubts the remaining elements of the population had had about the wisdom of the War of Independence were largely washed away by this protest campaign. It marked the effective unification of the Irish people, and simultaneously made the British position untenable.

The presence of troops, armored vehicles, and police in large numbers on the streets was a common feature of Irish daily life in the main centers of population during the period 1918–1922.

VII. The Mistake of Ireland

HERE IS ONE PHRASE WHICH CERTAIN IRISHMEN sometimes use in conversation, which indicates the real mistake that they sometimes make in controversy. When the more bitter sort of Irishman is at last convinced of the existence of the less bitter sort of Englishman, who does realize that he ought not to rule a Christian people by alternations of broken heads and broken promises, the Irishman has sometimes a way of saying, "I am sure you must have Irish blood in your veins." Several people told me so when I denounced Irish conscription, a thing ruinous to the whole cause of the Alliance. Some told me so even when I recalled the vile story of '98;[91] a thing damned by the whole opinion of the world. I assured them in vain that I did not need to have Irish blood in my veins, in order to object to having Irish blood on my hands. So far as I know, I have not one single drop of Irish blood in my veins. I have some Scottish blood; and some which, judging merely by a name in the family, must once have been French blood. But the determining part of it is purely English, and I believe East Anglian, at the flattest and farthest extreme from the Celtic fringe. But I am here concerned, not with whether it is true, but with why they should want to prove it is true. One would think they would want to prove precisely the opposite. Even if they were exaggerative and unscrupulous, they should surely seek to show that an Englishman was forced to condemn England, rather than that an Irishman was inclined to support Ireland. As it is, they are labouring to destroy the impartiality and even the independence of their own witness. It does not support, but rather surrenders Irish rights, to say that only the Irish can see that there are Irish wrongs. It is confessing that

Ireland is a Celtic dream and delusion, a cloud of sunset mistaken for an island. It is admitting that such a nation is only a notion, and a nonsensical notion; but in reality it is this notion about Irish blood that is nonsensical. Ireland is not an illusion; and her wrongs are not the subjective fancies of the Irish. Irishmen did not dream that they were evicted out of house and home by the ruthless application of a land law no man now dares to defend. It was not a nightmare that dragged them from their beds; nor were they sleepwalkers when they wandered as far as America. Skeffington did not have a delusion that he was being shot for keeping the peace; the shooting was objective, as the Prussian professors would say; as objective as the Prussian militarists could desire. The delusions were admittedly peculiar to the British official whom the British Government selected to direct operations on so important an occasion. I could understand it if the Imperialists took refuge in the Celtic cloud, conceived Colthurst as full of a mystic frenzy like the chieftain who fought with the sea, pleaded that Piggott was a poet whose pen ran away with him, or that Sergeant Sheridan romanced like a real stage Irishman. I could understand it if they declared that it was merely in the elvish ecstasy described by Mr. Yeats that Sir Edward Carson, that famous First Lord of the Admiralty, rode on the top of the dishevelled wave; and Mr. Walter Long,[92] that great Agricultural Minister, danced upon the mountains like a flame. It is far more absurd to suggest that no man can see the green flag unless he has some green in his eye. In truth this association between an Irish sympathy and an Irish ancestry is just as insulting as the old jibe of Buckingham, about an Irish interest or an Irish understanding.

    It may seem fanciful to say of the Irish nationalists that they are sometimes too Irish to be national. Yet this is really the case in those who would turn nationality from a sanctity to a secret. That is, they are turning it from something which everyone else ought to respect, to something which no one else can understand. Nationalism is a nobler thing even than patriotism; for nationalism appeals to a law of nations; it implies that a nation is a normal thing, and therefore one of a number of normal things. It is impossible to have a nation without Christendom; as it is impossible to have a citizen

The Mistake of Ireland

without a city. Now normally speaking this is better understood in Ireland than in England; but the Irish have an opposite exaggeration and error, and tend in some cases to the cult of real insularity. In this sense it is true to say that the error is indicated in the very name of Sinn Fein. But I think it is even more encouraged, in a cloudier and therefore more perilous fashion, by much that is otherwise valuable in the cult of the Celts and the study of the old Irish language. It is a great mistake for a man to defend himself as a Celt when he might defend himself as an Irishman. For the former defence will turn on some tricky question of temperament, while the latter will turn on the central pivot of morals. Celticism, by itself, might lead to all the racial extravagances which have lately led more barbaric races a dance. Celts also might come to claim, not that their nation is a normal thing, but that their race is a unique thing. Celts also might end by arguing not for an equality founded on the respect for boundaries, but for an aristocracy founded on the ramifications of blood. Celts also might come to pitting the prehistoric against the historic, the heathen against the Christian, and in that sense the barbaric against the civilized. In that sense I confess I do not care about the Celts; they are too like Teutons.

Now of course everyone knows that there is practically no such danger of Celtic Imperialism. Mr. Lloyd George[93] will not attempt to annex Brittany as a natural part of Britain. No Tories, however antiquated, will extend their empire in the name of the True Blue of the Ancient Britons. Nor is there the least likelihood that the Irish will overrun Scotland on the plea of an Irish origin for the old name of the Scots; or that they will set up an Irish capital at Stratford-on-Avon merely because *avon* is the Celtic word for water. That is the sort of thing that Teutonic ethnologists do; but the Celts are not quite so stupid as that, even when they are ethnologists. It may be suggested that this is because even prehistoric Celts seem to have been rather more civilized than historic Teutons. And indeed I have seen ornaments and utensils in the admirable Dublin museum, suggestive of a society of immense antiquity, and much more advanced in the arts of life than the Prussians were, only a few centuries ago. For instance, there was something that looked like a sort of safety razor. I doubt if the godlike Goths had much use for a razor; or if they had, if it was altogether safe. Nor am I so dull as not to be stirred of modern Irish poetry to praise this primordial and mysterious order, even as a sort of pagan paradise; and that not as regarding a legend as a sort of lie, but a tradition as a sort of truth. It is but another hint of a suggestion, huge yet hidden, that civilization is older than barbarism; and that the farther we go back into pagan origins, the nearer we come to the great Christian origin of the Fall. But whatever credit or sympathy be due to the cult of the Celtic origins in its proper place, it is none of these things that really prevents Celticism from being a barbarous imperialism like Teutonism. The thing that prevents imperialism is nationalism. It was exactly because Germany was not a nation that it desired more and more to be an empire. For a patriot is a sort of lover, and a lover is a sort of artist; and the artist will always love a shape too much to wish it to grow shapeless, even in order to grow large. A group of Teutonic tribes will not care how many other tribes they destroy or absorb; and Celtic tribes when they were heathen may have acted, for all I know, in the same way. But the civilized Irish nation, a part and product of Christendom, has certainly no desire to be entangled with other tribes, or to have its outlines blurred with great blots like Liverpool and Glasgow, as well as Belfast. In that sense it is far too self-conscious to be selfish. Its individuality may, as I shall suggest, make it too insular; it will not make it too imperial. This is a merit in nationalism too little noted; that even what is called its narrowness is not merely a barrier to invasion, but a barrier to expansion. Therefore, with all respect to the prehistoric Celts, I feel more at home with the good if sometimes mad Christian gentlemen of the Young Ireland[94] movement, or even the Easter Rebellion. I should feel more safe with Meagher of the Sword[95] than with the primitive Celt of the safety razor. The microscopic meanness of the Mid-Victorian English writers, when they wrote about Irish patriots, could see nothing but a very small joke in modern rebels thinking themselves worthy to take the titles of antique kings. But the only doubt I should have, if I had any, is whether the heathen kings were worthy of the Christian rebels. I am much more sure of the heroism of the modern Fenians than of the ancient ones.

Of the artistic side of the cult of the Celts I do not especially speak here. And indeed its importance, especially to the Irish, may easily be exaggerated. Mr. W. B. Yeats long ago dissociated himself from a merely racial theory of Irish poetry; and Mr. W. B. Yeats thinks as hard as he talks. I often entirely disagree with him; but I disagree more with the people who find him a poetical opiate, where I always find him a logical stimulant. For the rest, Celticism in some aspects is largely a conspiracy for leading the Englishman a dance, if it be a fairy dance. I suspect that many names and announcements are printed in Gaelic, not because Irishmen can read them, but because Englishmen can't. The other great modern mystic in Dublin, entertained us first by telling an English lady present that she would never resist the Celtic atmosphere, struggle how she might, but would soon be wandering in the mountain mists with a fillet round her head; which fate had apparently overtaken the son or nephew of an Anglican bishop who had strayed into those parts. The English lady, whom I happen to know rather well, made the characteristic announcement that she would go to Paris when she felt it coming on. But it seemed to me that such drastic action was hardly necessary, and that there was comparatively little cause for alarm; seeing that the mountain mists certainly had not had the effect on the people who happen to live in the mountains. I knew that the poet knew, even better than I did, that the Irish peasants do not wander about in fillets, or indeed wander about at all, having plenty of much better work to do. And since the Celtic atmosphere had no perceptible effect on the Celts, I felt no alarm about its effect on the Saxons. But the only thing involved, by way of an effect on the Saxons, was a practical joke on the Saxons; which may, however, have lasted longer in the case of the bishop's son than it did in mine. Anyhow, I continued to move about (like Atalanta in Calydon)[96] with unchapleted hair, with unfilleted cheek; and found sufficient number of Irish people in the same condition to prevent me from feeling shy. In a word, all that sort of thing is simply the poet's humour, especially his good humour, which is of a golden and godlike sort. And a man would be very much misled by the practical joke if he does not realize that the joker is a practical man. On the desk in front of him as he spoke were business papers of reports and statistics, much more concerned with fillets of veal than fillets of vision. That is the essential fact about all this side of such men in Ireland. We may think the Celtic ghost a turnip ghost; but we can only doubt the reality of the ghost; there is no doubt of the reality of the turnip.

But if the Celtic pose be a piece of the Celtic ornament, the spirit that produced it does also produce some more serious tendencies to the segregation of Ireland, one might almost say the secretion of Ireland. In this sense it is true that there is too much separatism in Ireland. I do not speak of separation from England, which, as I have said, happened long ago in the only serious sense, and is a condition to be assumed, not a conclusion to be avoided. Nor do I mean separation from some federation of free states including England; for that is a conclusion that could still be avoided with a little common sense and common honesty in our own politics. I mean separation from Europe, from the common Christian civilization by whose law the nations live. I would be understood as speaking here of exceptions rather than the rule; for the rule is rather the other way. The Catholic religion, the most fundamental fact in Ireland, is itself a permanent communication with the Continent. So, as I have said, is the free peasantry which is so often the economic expression of the same Faith. Mr. James Stephens, himself a spiritually detached man of genius, told me with great humour a story which is also at least a symbol. A Catholic priest, after a convivial conversation and plenty of good wine, said to him confidentially: "You ought to be a Catholic. You can be saved without being a Catholic; but you can't be Irish without being a Catholic."

Nevertheless, the exceptions are large enough to be dangers; and twice lately, I think, they have brought Ireland into danger. This is the age of minorities; of groups that rule rather than represent. And the two largest parties in Ireland, though more representative than most parties in England, were too much affected, I fancy, by the modern fashion, expressed in the world of fads by being Celtic rather than Catholic. They were just a little too insular to accept the old unconscious wave of Christendom: the Crusade. But the case was more extraordinary than that. They were even too insular to

The Mistake of Ireland

appreciate, not so much their own international needs, as their own international importance. It may seem a strange paradox to say that both nationalist parties underrated Ireland as a nation. It may seem a startling paradox to say that in this the most nationalist was the least national. Yet I think I can explain, however roughly, what I mean by saying that this is so.

It is primarily Sinn Fein, or the extreme national party, which thus relatively failed to realize that Ireland is a nation. At least it failed in nationalism exactly so far as it failed to intervene in the war of the nations against Prussian imperialism. For its argument involved, unconsciously, the proposition that Ireland is not a nation; that Ireland is a tribe or a settlement, or a chance sprinkling of aborigines. If the Irish were savages oppressed by the British Empire, they might well be indifferent to the fate of the British Empire; but as they were civilized men, they could not be indifferent to the fate of civilization. The Kaffirs[97] might conceivably be better off if the whole system of white colonization, Boer and British, broke down and disappeared altogether. The Irish might sympathize with the Kaffirs, but they would not like to be classed with the Kaffirs. Hottentots[98] might have a sort of Hottentot happiness if the last European city had fallen in ruins, or the last European had died in torments. But the Irish would never be Hottentots, even if they were pro-Hottentots. In other words, if the Irish were what Cromwell thought they were, they might well confine their attention to Hell and Connaught,[99] and have no sympathy to spare for France. But if the Irish are what Wolfe Tone[100] thought they were, they must be interested in France, as he was interested in France. In short, if the Irish are barbarians, they need not trouble about other barbarians sacking the cities of the world; but if they are citizens, they must trouble about the cities that are sacked. This is the deep and real reason why their alienation from the Allied cause was a disaster for their own national cause. It was not because it gave fools a chance of complaining that they were anti-English, it was because it gave much cleverer people the chance of complaining that they were anti-European. I entirely agree that the alienation was chiefly the fault of the English government; I even agree that it required an abnormal imaginative magnanimity for an Irishman to do his duty to Ireland, in spite of being so insolently told to do it. But it is nonetheless true that Ireland today would be ten thousand miles nearer her deliverance if the Irishman could have made that effort; if he had realized that the thing ought to be done, not because such rulers wanted it, but rather although they wanted it.

But the much more curious fact is this. There were any number of Irishmen, and those amongst the most Irish, who did realize this; who realized it with so sublime a sincerity as to fight

DAVID LLOYD GEORGE (1863–1946)

"The loss of justice for Ireland was simply a part of the loss of justice in England; the loss of all moral authority in government, the loss of the popularity of Parliament, the secret plutocracy which makes it easy to take a bribe or break a pledge, the corruption that can pass unpopular laws or promote discredited men."

for their own enemies against the world's enemies, and consent at once to be insulted by the English and killed by the Germans. The Redmonds and the old Nationalist party, if they have indeed failed, have the right to be reckoned among the most heroic of all the heroic failures of Ireland. If theirs is a lost cause, it is wholly worthy of a land where lost causes are never lost. But the old guard of Redmond did also in its time, I fancy, fall into the same particular and curious error, but in a more subtle way and on a seemingly remote subject.

The Mistake of Ireland

They also, whose motives like those of the Sinn Feiners were entirely noble, did in one sense fail to be national, in the sense of appreciating the international importance of the nation. In their case it was a matter of English and not European politics; and as their case was much more complicated, I speak with much less confidence about it. But I think there was a highly determining time in politics when certain Irishmen got on to the wrong side in English politics, as other Irishmen afterwards got on to the wrong side in European politics. And by the wrong side, in both cases, I not only mean the side that

SIR EDWARD HENRY CARSON
LORD OF DUNCAIRN (1854–1935)

"The political conventions that allow of dealing in Marconis at one price, are conventions that also allow of telling one story to Mr. John Redmond and another to Sir Edward Carson."

was not consistent with the truth, but the side that was not really congenial to the Irish. A man may act against the body, even the main body, of his nation; but if he acts against the soul of his nation, even to save it, he and his nation suffer.

I can best explain what I mean by reaffirming the reality which an English visitor really found in Irish politics, towards the end of the war. It may seem odd to say that the most hopeful fact I found, for Anglo-Irish relations, was the fury with which the Irish were all accusing the English of perjury and treason. Yet this was my solid and sincere impression; the happiest omen was the hatred aroused by the disappointment over Home Rule. For men are not furious unless they are disappointed of something they really want; and men are not disappointed except about something they were really ready to accept. If Ireland had been entirely in favour of entire separation, the loss of Home Rule would not be felt as a loss, but if anything as an escape. But it is felt bitterly and savagely as a loss; to that at least I can testify with entire certainty. I may or may not be right in the belief I build on it; but I believe it would still be felt as a gain; that Dominion Home Rule would in the long run satisfy Ireland. But it would satisfy her if it were given to her, not if it were promised to her. As it is, the Irish regard our Government simply as a liar who has broken his word; I cannot express how big and black that simple idea bulks in the landscape and blocks up the road. And without professing to regard it as quite so simple, I regard it as substantially true. It is, upon my argument, an astounding thing the Kings, Lords and Commons of a great nation should record on its statute book that a law exists, and then illegally reverse it in answer to the pressure of private persons. It is, and must be, for the people benefited by the law, an act of treason. The Irish were not wrong in thinking it an act of treason, even in the sense of treachery and trickery. Where they were wrong, I regret to say, was in talking of it as if it were the one supreme solitary example of such trickery; when the whole of our politics were full of such tricks. In short, the loss of justice in Ireland was simply a part of the loss of justice in England; the loss of all moral authority in government, the loss of the popularity of Parliament, the secret plutocracy which makes it easy to take a bribe or break a pledge, the corruption that can pass unpopular laws or promote discredited men. The law-giver cannot enforce his law because, whether or no the law be popular, the law-giver is wholly unpopular, and is perpetually passing wholly unpopular laws. Intrigue has been substituted for government; and the public man cannot appeal to the public because all the most important part of his policy is conducted in private. The modern politician conducts his public life in private. He sometimes condescends to make up for it by affecting to conduct his private life in public. He will put his baby or his birthday book into the illustrated papers; it is his dealings with the colossal millions of the cosmopolitan millionaires that he puts in his pocket or his private safe. We are allowed to know all about his dogs and cats; but not about those larger and more dangerous animals, his bulls and bears.

Now there was a moment when England had an opportunity of breaking down this parliamentary evil, as Europe afterwards had an opportunity (which it fortunately took) of breaking down the Prussian evil. The corruption was common to both parties; but the chance of exposing it happened to occur under the rule of a Home Rule party; which the Nationalists supported solely for the sake of Home Rule. In the Marconi Case they consented to whitewash the tricks of Jew jobbers whom they must have despised, just as some of the Sinn Feiners afterwards consented to whitewash the wickedness of Prussian bullies whom they also must have despised. In both cases the motive was wholly disinterested and even idealistic. It was the practicality that was unpractical. I was one of a small group which protested against the hushing up of the Marconi affair,[101] but we always did justice to the patriotic intentions of the Irish who allowed it. But we based our criticism of their strategy on the principle of *falsus in uno, falsus in omnibus*.[102] The man who will cheat you about one thing will cheat you about another. The men who will lie to you about Marconi, will lie to you about Home Rule. The political conventions that allow of dealing in Marconis at one price for the party, and another price for oneself, are conventions that also allow of telling one story to Mr. John Redmond[103] and another to Sir Edward Carson. The man who will imply one state of things when talking at large in Parliament, and another state of things when put into a witness box in court, is the same sort of man who will promise an Irish settlement in the hope that it may fail; and then withdraw it for fear it should succeed. Among the many muddle-headed modern attempts to coerce the Christian poor to the Moslem dogma about wine and beer, one was concerned with abuse by loafers or tipplers of the privilege of the Sunday traveller. It was suggested that the travellers' claims were in every sense travellers' tales. It was therefore proposed that the limit of three miles should be extended to six; as if it were any harder for a liar to say he had walked six miles than three. The politicians might be as ready to promise to walk the six miles to an Irish Republic as the three miles to an Irish Parliament. But Sinn Fein is mistaken in supposing that any change of theoretic claim meets the problem of corruption. Those who would break their word to Redmond would certainly break it to De Valera.[104] We urged all these things on the Nationalists whose national cause we supported; we asked them to follow their larger popular instincts, break down a corrupt oligarchy, and let a real popular parliament in England give a real popular parliament in Ireland. With entirely honourable motives, they adhered to the narrower conception of their national duty. They sacrificed everything for Home Rule, even their own profoundly national emotion of contempt. For the sake of Home Rule, they kept such men in power; and for their reward they found that such men were still in power; and Home Rule was gone.

What I mean about the Nationalist Party, and what may be called its prophetic shadow of the Sinn Fein mistake, may well be symbolized in one of the noblest figures of that party or any party. An Irish poet, talking to me about the pointed diction of the Irish peasant, said he had recently rejoiced in the society of a drunken Kerry farmer, whose conversation was a litany of questions about everything in heaven and earth, each ending with a sort of chorus of "Will ye tell me that now?" And at the end of all he said abruptly, "Did you know Tom Kettle?," and on my friend the poet assenting, the farmer said, as if in triumph, "And why are so many people alive that ought to be dead, and so many people dead that ought to be alive. Will ye tell me that now?" That is not unworthy of an old heroic poem, and therefore not unworthy of the hero and poet of whom it was spoken. "Patroclus died, who was a better man than you." Thomas Michael Kettle was perhaps the greatest example of that greatness of spirit which was so ill-rewarded on both sides of the channel and of the quarrel, which marked Redmond's brother and so many of Redmond's followers. He was a wit, a scholar, an orator, a man ambitious in all the arts of peace; and he fell fighting the barbarians because he was too good a European to use the barbarians against England, as England a hundred years before had used the barbarians against Ireland. There is nothing to be said of such

The Mistake of Ireland

things except what the drunken farmer said, unless it be a verse from a familiar ballad on a very remote topic, which happens to express my own most immediate feelings about politics and reconstruction after the decimation of the Great War.

> The many men so beautiful
> And they all dead did lie:
> And a thousand thousand slimy things
> Lived on, and so did I.

It is not a reflection that adds any inordinate self-satisfaction to the fact of one's own survival.

In turning over a collection of Kettle's extraordinarily varied and vigorous writings, which contain some of the most pointed and piercing criticisms of materialism, of modern Capitalism and mental and moral anarchism generally, I came on a very interesting criticism of myself and my friends in our Marconi agitation; a suggestion, on a note of genial cynicism, that we were asking for an impossible political purity; a suggestion which, knowing it to be patriotic, I will venture to call pathetic. I will not now return on such disagreements with a man with whom I so universally agree; but it will not be unfair to find here an exact illustration of what I mean by saying that the national leaders, so far from merely failing as wild Irishmen, only failed when they were not instinctive enough, that is, not Irish enough. Kettle was a patriot whose impulse was practical, and whose policy was impolitic. Here also the Nationalist underrated the importance of the intervention of his own nationality. Kettle left a fine and even terrible poem, asking if his sacrifices were in vain, and whether he and his people were again being betrayed. I think nobody can deny that he was betrayed; but it was not by the English soldiers with whom he marched to war, but by those very English politicians with whom he sacrificed so much to remain at peace. No man will ever dare to say his death in battle was in vain, not only because in the highest sense it could never be, but because even in the lowest sense it was not. He hated the icy insolence of Prussia; and that ice is broken, and already as weak as water. As Carlyle said of a far lesser thing, that at least will never though unending ages insult the face of the sun any more.[105] The point is here that if any part of his fine work was in vain, it was certainly not the reckless romantic part; it was precisely the plodding parliamentary part. None can say that the weary marching and counter-marching in France was a thing thrown away; not only in the sense which consecrates all footprints along such a *via crucis*, or highway of the army of martyrs; but also in the perfectly practical sense, that the army was going somewhere, and that it got there. But it might possibly be said that the weary marching and counter-marching at Westminster, in and out of a division lobby, belonged to what the French call the *salle des pas perdus*.[106] If anything was practical it was the visionary adventure; if anything was unpractical it was the practical compromise. He and his friends were betrayed by the men whose corruptions they had contemptuously condoned, far more than by the men whose bigotries they had indignantly denounced. There darkened about them treason and disappointment, and he that was the happiest died in battle; and one who knew and loved him spoke to me for a million others in saying: "And now we will not give you a dead dog until you keep your word."

A photo of the famous Mayo Flying Column of the IRA, taken on June 21, 1921. The Mayo Flying Column confronted 600 British troops at Tourmakeady in 1921 and inflicted heavy losses, while themselves loosing only a single man. The tactics of guerilla fighting practiced by the "Flying Columns" were developed as a result of painful lessons learned by the Irish of the 1916 and former rebellions, who, with poorly armed people's militias, attempted to confront trained, regular troops.

VIII. An Example and a Question

E ALL HAD OCCASION TO REJOICE AT THE RETURN of Sherlock Holmes when he was supposed to be dead; and I presume we may soon rejoice in his return even when he is really dead. Sir Arthur Conan Doyle,[107] in his widespread new campaign in favour of Spiritualism, ought at least to delight us with the comedy of Holmes as a control and Watson as a medium. But I have for the moment a use for the great detective not concerned with the psychical side of the question. Of that I will only say, in passing, that in this case as in many other cases, I find myself in agreement with an authority about where the line is drawn between good and bad, but have the misfortune to think his good bad, and his bad good. Sir Arthur explains why he would lift Spiritualism to a graver and more elevated plane of idealism; and that he quite agrees with his critics that the mere tricks with tables and chairs are grotesque and vulgar. I think this quite true if turned upside down, like the table. I do not mind the grotesque and vulgar part of Spiritualism; what I object to is the grave and elevating part. After all, a miracle is a miracle and means something; it means that Materialism is nonsense. But it is not true that a message is always a message; and it sometimes only means that Spiritualism is also nonsense. If the table at which I am now writing takes to itself wings and flies out of the window, perhaps carrying me along with it, the incident will arouse in me a real intelligent interest, verging on surprise. But if the pen with which I am writing begins to scrawl, all by itself, the sort of things I have seen in spirit writing; if it begins to say that all things are aspects of universal purity and peace, and so on, why, then I shall not only be annoyed, but also bored. If a great man like

the late Sir William Crookes[108] says a table went walking upstairs, I am impressed by the news; but not by news from nowhere to the effect that all men are perpetually walking upstairs, up a spiritual staircase, which seems to be as mechanical and labour-saving as a moving staircase at Charing Cross.[109] Moreover, even a benevolent spirit might conceivably throw the furniture about merely for fun; whereas I doubt if anything but a devil from hell would say that all things are aspects of purity and peace.

But I am here taking from the Spiritualistic articles a text that has nothing to do with Spiritualism. In a recent contribution to *Nash's Magazine*,[110] Sir Arthur Conan Doyle remarks very truly that the modern world is weary and wicked and in need of a religion; and he gives examples of its more typical and terrible corruptions. It is perhaps natural that he should revert to the case of the Congo, and talk of it in the torrid fashion which recalls the days when Morel[111] and Casement had some credit in English politics. We have since had an opportunity of judging the real attitude of a man like Morel in the plainest case of black and white injustice that the world has ever seen. It was at once a replica and a reversal of the position expressed in the Pious Editor's Creed,[112] and might roughly be rendered in similar language.

> I do believe in Freedom's cause
> Ez fur away ez tropics are;
> But Belgians caught in Prussia's claws
> To me less tempting topics are.
> It's wal agin a foreign king
> To rouse the chapel's rigours;
> But Liberty's a kind of thing
> We only owe to niggers.

He had of course a lurid denunciation of the late King Leopold, of which I will only say that, uttered by a Belgian about the Belgian king in his own land and lifetime, it would be highly courageous and largely correct; but that the parallel test is how much truth was told by British journalists about British kings in their own land and lifetime; and that until we can pass the test, such denunciations do us very little good. But what interests me in the matter at the moment is this. Sir Arthur feels it right to say something about British corruptions, and passes from the Congo to Putumayo, touching a little more lightly; for even the most honest Britons have an unconscious trick of touching more lightly on the case of British capitalists. He says that our capitalists were not guilty of direct cruelty, but of an attitude careless and even callous. But what strikes me is that Sir Arthur, with his taste for such protests and inquiries, need not have wandered quite so far from his own home as the forests of South America.

Sir Arthur Conan Doyle is an Irishman; and in his own country, within my own memory, there occurred a staggering and almost incredible crime, or series of crimes, which were worthier than anything in the world of the attention of Sherlock Holmes in fiction, or Conan Doyle in reality. It always will be a tribute to the author of *Sherlock Holmes* that he did, about the same time, do such good work in reality. He made an admirable plea for Adolf Beck[113] and Oscar Slater;[114] he was also connected, I remember, with the reversal of a miscarriage of justice in a case of cattle mutilation. And all this, while altogether to his credit, makes it seem all the more strange that his talents could not be used for, and in, his own home and native country, in a mystery that had the dimensions of a monstrosity, and which did involve, if I remember right, a question of cattle-maiming. Anyhow, it was concerned with moonlighters and the charges made against them, such as the common one of cutting off the tails of cows. I can imagine Sherlock Holmes on such a quest, keen-eyed and relentless, finding the cloven hoof of some sinister and suspected cow. I can imagine Dr. Watson, like the cow's tail, always behind. I can imagine Sherlock Holmes remarking, in a light allusive fashion, that he himself had written a little monograph on the subject of cows tails; with diagrams and tables solving the great traditional problem of how many cows tails would reach the moon; a subject of extraordinary interest to moonlighters. And I can still more easily imagine him saying afterwards, having resumed the pipe and dressing gown of Baker Street, "A remarkable little problem, Watson. In some of its features it was perhaps more singular than any you have been good enough to report. I do not think that even the Tooting Trouser-Stretching Mystery, or the singular little affair of the Radium Toothpick, offered more strange and sensational developments." For if the celebrated pair had really tracked out the Irish crime I have in mind, they would have found a story which, considered merely as a detective story, is by far the most dramatic and dreadful of modern times. Like nearly all such sensational stories, it traced the crime to somebody far higher in station and responsibility than any of those suspected. Like many of the most sensational of them, it actually traced the crime to the detective who was investigating it. For if they had really crawled about with a magnifying glass, studying the supposed footprints of the peasants incriminated, they would have found they were made by the boots of the policeman. And the boots of the policeman, one feels, are things that even Watson might recognize.

I have told the astounding story of Sergeant Sheridan before; and I shall often tell it again. Hardly any English people know it; and I shall go on telling it in the hope that all English people may know it some day. It ought to be first in every collection of *causes célèbres*, in every book about criminals, in every book of historical mysteries; and on its merits it would be. It is not in any of them. It is not there because there is a motive, in all modern British plutocracy, against finding the big British miscarriages of justice where they are really to be found; and that is a great deal nearer than Putumayo.[115] It is a place far more appropriate to the exploits of the family of the Doyles. It is called Ireland; and in that place a powerful British official named Sheridan had been highly successful in the imperial service by convicting a series of poor Irishmen of agrarian crimes. It was afterwards discovered that the British official had carefully committed every one of the crimes himself; and then, with equal foresight, perjured himself to imprison innocent men. Any one who does not know the story will naturally ask what punishment was held adequate for such a Neronian monster; I will tell him. He was bowed out of the country like a distinguished stranger, his expenses politely paid, as if he had been delivering a series of instructive lectures; and he is now probably smoking a cigar in an American hotel, and much more comfortable than any poor policeman who has done his duty. I defy anybody to deny him a place in our literature about great criminals. Charles Peace[116] escaped many times before conviction; Sheridan escaped altogether after conviction. Jack the Ripper[117] was safe because he was undiscovered; Sheridan was discovered and was still safe. But I only repeat the matter here for two reasons. First, we may call our rule in Ireland what we like; we may call it the union when there is no union; we may call it Protestant ascendancy when we are no longer Protestants; or Teutonic lordship when we could only be ashamed of being Teutons. But this is what it is, and everything else is waste of words. And second, because an Irish investigator of cattle-maiming, so oblivious of the Irish cow, is in some danger of figuring as an Irish bull.

Anyhow, that is the real and remarkable story of Sergeant Sheridan, and I put it first because it is the most practical test of the practical question of whether Ireland is misgoverned. It is strictly a fair test; for it is a test by the minimum and an argument *a fortiori*. A British official in Ireland can run a career of crime, punishing innocent people for his own felonies, and when he is found out, he is found to be above the law. This may seem like putting things at the worst, but it is really putting them at the best. This story was not told us on the word of a wild Irish Fenian, or even a responsible Irish Nationalist. It was told, word for word as I have told it, by the Unionist Minister in charge of the matter and reporting it, with regret and shame, to Parliament. He was not one of the worst Irish Secretaries, who might be responsible for the worst *régime*; on the contrary, he was by far the best. If even he could only partially restrain or reveal such things, there can be no deduction in common sense except that in the ordinary way such things go on daily in the dark with nobody to reveal and nobody to restrain them. It was not something done in those dark days of torture and terrorism, which happened in Ireland a hundred years ago, and which Englishmen talk of as having happened a million years ago. It was something that happened quite recently, in my own mature manhood, about the time that the better things like the Land Acts were already before the world. I remember writing to the *Westminster Gazette*[118] to emphasize it when it occurred; but it seems to have passed out of memory in an almost half-witted fashion. But that peep-hole into hell has afforded me ever since a horrible amusement, when I hear the Irish softly rebuked for remembering old unhappy far-off things and wrongs done in the Dark Ages. Thus I was especially amused to find the Rev. R.J. Campbell[119] saying that "Ireland has been petted and coddled more than any other part of the British Isles"; because Mr. Campbell was chiefly famous for a comfortable creed himself, for saying that evil is only "a shadow where light should be"; and there is no doubt here of his throwing a very black shadow where light is very much required. I will conceive the policeman at the corner of the street in which Mr. Campbell resides as in the habit of killing a crossing-sweeper every now and then for his private entertainment, burgling the houses of Mr. Campbell's neighbours, cutting off the tails of their carriage horses, and otherwise disporting himself by moonlight like a fairy. It is his custom to visit the consequences of each of these crimes upon the Rev. R.J. Campbell, whom he arrests at intervals, successfully convicts by perjury, and proceeds to coddle in penal servitude. But I have another reason for mentioning Mr. Campbell, a gentleman whom I heartily respect in many other respects; and the reason is connected with his name, as it occurs in another connection on another page. It shows how in anything, but especially in anything coming from Ireland, the old facts of family and Faith outweigh a million modern philosophies. The words in *Who's Who* – "Ulster Protestant of Scottish ancestry" – give the really Irish and the really honourable reason for Mr. Campbell's extraordinary remark. A man may preach for years, with radiant universalism, that many waters cannot quench love; but Boyne Water[120] can. Mr. Campbell appears very promptly with what Kettle called "a bucketful of Boyne, to put the sunrise out."[21] I will not take the opportunity of saying, like the Ulsterman, that there never was treason yet but a Campbell was at the bottom of it. But I will say that there never was Modernism yet but a Calvinist was at the bottom of it. The old theology is much livelier than the New Theology.

Many other such true tales could be told; but what we need here is a sort of test. This tale is a test; because it is the best that could

An Example and a Question

be said, about the best that could be done, by the best Englishman ruling Ireland, in face of the English system established here; and it is the best, or at any rate the most, that we can know about that system. Another truth which might also serve as a test, is this; to note among the responsible English not only their testimony against each other, but their testimony against themselves. I mean the consideration of how very rapidly we realize that our own conduct in Ireland has been infamous, not in the remote past, but in the very recent past. I have lived just long enough to see the wheel come full circle inside one generation; when I was a schoolboy, the sort of Kensington middle class to which I belong was nearly solidly resisting, not only the first Home Rule Bill, but any suggestion that the Land League[122] had a leg to stand on, or that the landlords need do anything but get their rents or kick out their tenants. The whole Unionist Press, which was three-quarters of the Press, simply supported Clanricarde,[123] and charged anyone who did not do so with supporting the Clan-na-Gael.[124] Mr. Balfour[125] was simply admired for enforcing the system, which it is his real apologia to have tried to end, or at least to have allowed Wyndham to end. I am not yet far gone in senile decay; but already I have lived to hear my countrymen talk about their own blind policy in the time of the Land League, exactly as they talked before of their blind policy in the time of the Limerick Treaty.[126] The shadow on our past, shifts forward as we advance into the future; and always seems to end just behind us. I was told in my youth that the age-long misgovernment of Ireland lasted down to about 1870; it is now agreed among all intelligent people that it lasted at least down to about 1890. A little common sense, after a hint like the Sheridan case, will lead one to suspect the simple explanation that it is going on still.

Now I heard scores of such stories as the Sheridan story in Ireland, many of which I mention elsewhere; but I do not mention them here because they cannot be publicly tested; and that for a very simple reason. We must accept all the advantages and disadvantages of a rule of absolute and iron militarism. We cannot impose silence and then sift stories; we cannot forbid argument and then ask for proof; we cannot destroy rights and then discover wrongs. I say this quite impartially in the matter of militarism itself. I am far from certain that soldiers are worse rulers than lawyers and merchants; and I am quite certain that a nation has a right to give abnormal power to its soldiers in time of war. I only say that a soldier, if he is a sensible soldier, will know what he is doing and therefore what he cannot do; that he cannot gag a man then cross-examine him, any more than he can blow out his brains and then convince his intelligence. There may be; humanly speaking, there must be, a mass of injustices in the militaristic government of Ireland. The militarism itself may be the least of them; but it must involve the concealment of all the rest.

It has been remarked above that establishing militarism is a thing which a nation had a right to do, and (what is not at all the same thing) which it may be right in doing. But with that very phrase "a nation," we collide of course with the whole real question; the alleged abstract wrong about which the Irish talk much more than about their concrete wrongs. I have put first the matters mentioned above, because I wish to make clear, as a matter of common sense, the impression of any reasonable outsider that they certainly have concrete wrongs. But even those who doubt it, and say that the Irish have no concrete grievance but only a sentiment of Nationalism, fall into a final and very serious error about the nature of the thing called Nationalism, and even the meaning of the word "concrete." For the truth is that, in dealing with a nation, the grievance which is most abstract of all is also the one which is most concrete of all.

Not only is patriotism a part of practical politics, but it is more practical than any politics. To neglect it, and ask only for grievances, is like counting the clouds and forgetting the climate. To neglect it, and think only of laws, is like seeing the landmarks and never seeing the landscape. It will be found that the denial of nationality is much more of a daily nuisance than the denial of votes or the denial of juries. Nationality is the most practical thing, because so many things are national without being political, or without being legal. A man in a conquered country feels it when he goes to market or even goes to church, which may be more often than he goes to law; and the harvest is more general than the General Election. Altering the flag on the roof is like altering the sun in the sky; the very chimney pots and lamp posts look different. Nay, after a certain interval of occupation they are different. As a man would know he was in a land of strangers before he knew it was a land of savages, so he knows a rule is alien long before he knows it is oppressive. It is not necessary for it to add injury to insult.

For instance, when I first walked about Dublin, I was disposed to smile at the names of the streets being inscribed in Irish as well as English. I will not here discuss the question of what is called the Irish language, the only arguable case against which is that it is not the Irish language. But at any rate it is not the English language, and I have come to appreciate more imaginatively the importance of that fact. It may be used rather as a weapon than a tool; but it is a national weapon if it is not a national tool. I see the significance of having something which the eye commonly encounters, as it does a chimney pot or a lamp post; but which is like a chimney reared above an Irish hearth or a lamp to light an Irish road. I see the point of having a solid object in the street to remind an Irishman that he is in Ireland, as a red pillar box reminds an Englishman that he is in England. But there must be a thousand things as practical as pillar boxes which remind an Irishman that, if he is in his country, it is not yet a free country; everything connected with the principal seat of government reminds him of it perpetually. It may not be easy for an Englishman to imagine how many of such daily details there are. But there is, after all, one very simple effort of the fancy, which would fix the fact for him forever. He has only to imagine that the Germans have conquered London.

A brilliant writer who has earned the name of a Pacifist, and even a pro-German, once propounded to me his highly personal and even perverse type of internationalism by saying, as a sort of unanswerable challenge, "Wouldn't you rather be ruled by Goethe than by Walter Long?" I replied that words could not express the wild love and loyalty I should feel for Mr. Walter Long, if the only alternative were Goethe. I could not have put my own national case in a clearer or more compact form. I might occasionally feel inclined to kill Mr. Long; but under the approaching shadow of Goethe, I should feel more inclined to kill myself. That is the deathly element in denationalisation; that it poisons life itself, the most real of all realities. But perhaps the best way of putting the point conversationally is to say that Goethe would certainly put up a monument to Shakespeare. I would sooner die than walk past it every day of my life. And in the other case of the street inscriptions, it is well to remember that these things, which we also walk past every day, are exactly the sort of things that always have, in a nameless fashion, the national note. If the Germans conquered London, they would not need to massacre me or even enslave me in order to annoy me; it would be quite enough that their notices were in a German style, if not in a German language. Suppose I looked up in an English railway carriage and saw these words written in English exactly as I have seen them in a German railway carriage written in German: "The outleaning of the body from the window of the carriage is because of the therewith bound up life's danger strictly prohibited." It is not rude. It would certainly be impossible to complain that it is curt. I should not be annoyed by its brutality and brevity; but on the contrary by its elaborateness and even its laxity. But if it does not exactly shine in lucidity, it gives a reason; which after all is a very reasonable thing to do. By every cosmopolitan test, it is more polite than the sentence I have read in my childhood: "Wait until the train stops." This is curt; this might be called rude; but it never annoyed me in the least. The nearest I can get to defining my sentiment is to say that I can sympathize with the Englishman who wrote the English notice. Having a rude thing to write, he wrote it as quickly as he could, and went home to his tea; or preferably to his beer. But what is too much for me, an overpowering vision, is the thought of that German calmly sitting down to compose that sentence like a sort of essay. It is the thought of him serenely waving away the one important word till the very end of the sentence, like the Day of Judgement to the end of the world. It is perhaps the mere thought that he did not break down in the middle of it, but endured to the end; or that he could afterwards calmly review it, and see that sentence go marching by, like the whole German army. In short, I do not object to it because it is dictatorial or despotic or bureaucratic or anything of the kind, but simply because it is German. Because it is German I do not object to it in Germany.

Because it is German I should violently revolt against it in England. I do not revolt against the command to wait until the train stops, not because it is less rude, but because it is the kind of rudeness I can understand. The official may be treating me casually, but at least he is not treating himself seriously. And so, in return, I can treat him and his notice not seriously but casually. I can neglect to wait until the train stops, and fall down on the platform, as I did on the platform of Wolverhampton, to the permanent damage of that fine structure. I can, by a stroke of satiric genius, truly national and traditional, the dexterous elimination of a single letter, alter the maxim to "Wait until the rain stops." It is a jest as profoundly English as the weather to which it refers. Nobody would be tempted to take such a liberty with the German sentence; not only because he would be instantly imprisoned in a fortress, but because he would not know at which end to begin.

Now this is the truth which is expressed, though perhaps very imperfectly, in things like the Gaelic lettering on streets in Dublin. It will be wholesome for us who are English to realize that there is almost certainly an English way of putting things, even the most harmless things, which appears to an Irishman quite as ungainly, unnatural and ludicrous as that German sentence appears to me. As the famous Frenchman did not know when he was talking prose, the official Englishman does not know when he is talking English. He unconsciously assumes that he is talking Esperanto. Imperialism is not an insanity of patriotism; it is merely an illusion of cosmopolitanism.

For the national note of the Irish language is not peculiar to what used to be called the Erse language. The whole nation used the tongue common to both nations with a difference far beyond a dialect. It is not a difference of accent, but a difference of style; which is generally a difference of soul. The emphasis, the elision, the short cuts and sharp endings of speech, show a variety which may be almost unnoticeable but is nonetheless untranslatable. It may be only a little more weight on a word, or an inversion allowable in English but abounding in Irish; but we can no more copy it than copy the compactness of the French *on* or the Latin ablative absolute.

The commonest case of what I mean, for instance, is the locution that lingers in my mind with an agreeable phrase from one of Mr. Yeats's stories: "Whom I shall yet see upon the hob of hell, and them screeching": It is an idiom that gives the effect of a pointed manuscript, a parting kick or sting in the tail of the sentence, which is unfathomably national. It is noteworthy and even curious that quite a crowd of Irishmen, who quoted to me with just admiration the noble ending of *Kathleen-na-Hulahan*,[127] where the newcomer is asked if he has seen the old woman who is the tragic type of Ireland going out, quoted his answer in that form, "I did not. But I saw a young woman, and she walking like a queen." I say it is curious, because I have since been told that in the actual book (which I cannot lay my hand on at the moment) a more classic English idiom is used. It would generally be most unwise to alter the diction of such a master of style as Mr. Yeats: though indeed it is possible that he altered it himself, as he has sometimes done, and not always, I think, for the better. But whether this form came from himself or from his countrymen, it was very redolent of his country. And there was something inspiring in thus seeing, as it were before one's eyes, literature becoming legend. But a hundred other examples could be given, even from my own short experience, of such fine turns of language, nor are the finest necessarily to be found in literature. It is perfectly true, though prigs may overwork and snobs underrate the truth, that in a country like this the peasants can talk like poets. When I was on the wild coast of Donegal, an old unhappy woman who had starved through the famines and the evictions, was telling a lady the tales of those times, and she mentioned quite naturally one that might have come straight out of times so mystical that we should call them mythical, that some travellers had met a poor wandering woman with a baby in those great grey rocky wastes, and asked her who she was. And she answered, "I am the Mother of God, and this is Himself, and He is the boy you will all be wanting at the last."

There is more in that story than can be put into any book, even on a matter in which its meaning plays so deep a part, and it seems almost profane to analyse it however sympathetically. But if anyone wishes to know what I mean by the untranslatable truth

An Example and a Question

which makes a language national, it will be worthwhile to look at the mere diction of that speech, and note how its whole effect turns on certain phrases and customs which happen to be peculiar to the nation. It is well know that in Ireland the husband or head of the house is always called "himself"; nor is it peculiar to the peasantry, but adopted, if partly in jest, by the gentry. A distinguished Dublin publicist, a landlord and leader among the more national aristocracy, always called me "himself" when he was talking to my wife. It will be noted how a sort of shadow of that common meaning mingles with the more shining significance of its position in a sentence where it is also strictly logical, in the sense of theological. All literary style, especially national style, is made up of such coincidences, which are a spiritual sort of puns. That is why style is untranslatable; because it is possible to render the meaning, but not the double meaning. There is even a faint differentiation in the half-humorous possibilities of the word "boy"; another wholly national nuance. Say instead, "And He is the Child," and it is something perhaps stiffer, and certainly quite different. Take away, "This is Himself" and simply substitute "This is He," and it is a piece of pedantry ten thousand miles from the original. But above all it has lost its note of something national, because it has lost its note of something domestic. All roads in Ireland, of fact or folklore, of theology or grammar, lead us back to that door and hearth of the household, that fortress of the family which is the key fortress of the whole strategy of the island. The Irish Catholics, like other Christians, admit a mystery in the Holy Trinity, but they may almost be said to admit an experience in the Holy Family. Their historical experience, alas, has made it seem to them not unnatural that the Holy Family should be a homeless family. They also have found that there was no room for them at the inn, or anywhere but in the jail; they also have dragged their newborn babes out of their cradles, and trailed in despair along the road to Egypt, or at least along the road to exile. They also have heard, in the dark and the distance behind them, the noise of the horsemen of Herod.

Now it is this sensation of stemming a stream, of ten thousand things all pouring one way, labels, titles, monuments, metaphors, modes of address, assumptions in controversy, that make an Englishman in Ireland know that he is in a strange land. Nor is he merely bewildered, as among a medley of strange things. On the contrary, if he has any sense, he soon finds them unified and simplified to a single impression, as if he were talking to a strange person. He cannot define it, because nobody can define a person, and nobody can define a nation. He can only see it, smell it, hear it, handle it, bump into it, fall over it, kill it, be killed for it, or be damned for doing it wrong. He must be content with these mere hints of its existence; but he cannot define it, because it is like a person, and no book of logic will undertake to define Aunt Jane or Uncle William. We can only say, with more or less mournful conviction, that if Aunt Jane is not a person, there is no such thing as a person. And I say with equal conviction that if Ireland is not a nation, there is no such thing as a nation. France is not a nation, England is not a nation; there is no such thing as patriotism on this planet. Any Englishman, of any party, with any proposal, may well clear his mind of cant about that preliminary question. If we free Ireland, we must free it to be a nation; if we go on repressing Ireland, we are repressing a nation; if we are right to repress Ireland, we are right to repress a nation. After that we may consider what can be done, according to our opinions about the respect due to patriotism, the reality of cosmopolitan and imperial alternatives, and so on. I will debate with the man who does not want mankind divided into nations at all; I can imagine a case for the man who wants specially to restrain anti-national Prussia. But I will not argue with a man about whether Ireland is a nation, or about the yet more awful question of whether it is an island. I know there is a sceptical philosophy which suggests that all ultimate ideas are only penultimate ideas, and therefore perhaps that all islands are really peninsulas. But I will claim to know what I mean by an island and what I mean by an individual; and when I think suddenly of my experience in the island in question, the impression is a single one; the voices mingle in a human voice which I should know if I heard it again, calling in the distance; the crowds dwindle into a single figure whom I have seen long ago upon a strange hillside, and she walking like a queen.

IX. Belfast and the Religious Problem

IF THAT CLOUD OF DREAM WHICH SEEMS TO DRIFT over so many Irish poems and impressions, I felt very little in Ireland. There is a real meaning in this suggestion of a mystic sleep, but it does not mean what most of us imagine, and it is not to be found where we expect it. On the contrary, I think the most vivid impression the nation left on me, was that it was almost unnaturally wide awake. I might almost say that Ireland suffers from insomnia. This is not only literally true, of those tremendous talks, the prolonged activities of rich and restless intellects, that can burn up the nights from darkness to daybreak. It is true on the doubtful as well as the delightful side, and the temperament has something of the morbid vigilance and even of the irritability of insomnia. Its lucidity is not only superhuman, but it is sometimes in the true sense inhuman. Its intellectual clarity cannot resist the temptation to intellectual cruelty. If I had to sum up in a sentence the one fault really to be found with the Irish, I could do it simply enough. I should say it saddened me that I liked them all so much better than they liked each other. But it is our supreme stupidity that this is always taken as meaning that Ireland is a sort of Donnybrook Fair.[128] It is really quite the reverse of a merely rowdy and irresponsible quarrel. So far from fighting with shillelaghs, they fight far too much with rapiers; their temptation is in the very nicety and even delicacy of the thrust. Of course there are multitudes who make no such deadly use of the national irony; but it is sufficiently common for even these to suffer from it; and after a time I began to understand a little that burden about bitterness of speech, which recurs so often in the songs of Mr. Yeats and other Irish poets.

> Though hope fall from you and love decay
> Burning in fires of a slanderous tongue.[129]

But there is nothing dreamy about the bitterness; the worst part of it is the fact that the criticisms always have a very lucid and logical touch of truth. It is not for us to lecture the Irish about forgiveness, who have given them so much to forgive. But if someone who had not lost the right to preach to them, if St. Patrick were to return to preach, he would find that nothing had failed, through all those ages of agony, of faith and honour and endurance; but I think he might possibly say, what I have no right to say, a word about charity.

There is indeed one decisive sense in which the Irish are very poetical; in that of giving a special and serious social recognition to poetry. I have sometimes expressed the fancy that men in the Golden Age might spontaneously talk in verse; and it is really true that half the Irish talk is in verse. Quotation becomes recitation. But it is much too rhythmic to resemble our own theatrical recitations. This is one of my own strongest and most sympathetic memories, and one of my most definable reasons for having felt extraordinarily happy in Dublin. It was a paradise of poets, in which a man who may feel inclined to mention a book or two of *Paradise Lost*,[130] or illustrate his meaning with the complete ballad of the *Ancient Mariner*,[131] feels he will be better understood than elsewhere. But the more this very national quality is noted, the less it will be mistaken for anything merely irresponsible, or even merely emotional. The shortest way of stating the truth is to say that poetry plays the part of music. It is in every sense of the phrase a social function. A poetical evening is as natural as a musical evening, and being as natural it becomes what is called artificial. As in some circles, "Do you play?" is rather "Don't you play?" these Irish circles would be surprised because a man did not recite rather than because he did. A hostile critic, especially an Irish critic, might possibly say that the Irish are poetical because they are not sufficiently musical. I can imagine Mr. Bernard Shaw saying something of the sort. But it might well be retorted that they are not merely musical because they will not consent to be merely emotional. It is far truer to say that they give a reasonable place to poetry, than that they permit any particular poetic interference with reason. "But I, whose virtues are the definitions of the analytical mind," says Mr. Yeats, and anyone who has been in the atmosphere will know what he means. Insofar as such things stray from reason, they tend rather to ritual than to riot. Poetry is in Ireland what humour is in America; it is an institution. The Englishman, who is always for good and evil the amateur, takes both in a more occasional and even accidental fashion. It must always be remembered here that the ancient Irish civilization had a high order of poetry, which was not merely mystical, but rather mathematical. Like Celtic ornament, Celtic verse tended too much to geometrical patterns. If this was irrational, it was not by excess of emotion. It might rather be described as irrational by excess of reason. The antique hierarchy of minstrels, each grade with its own complicated metre, suggests that there was something Chinese about a thing so inhumanly civilized. Yet all this vanished etiquette is somehow in the air in Ireland; and men and women move to it, as to the steps of a lost dance.

Thus, whether we consider the sense in which the Irish are really quarrelsome, or the sense in which they are really poetical, we find that both lead us back to a condition of clarity which seems the very reverse of a mere dream. In both cases Ireland is critical, and even self-critical. The bitterness I have ventured to lament is not Irish bitterness against the English; that I should assume as not only inevitable, but substantially justifiable. It is Irish bitterness against the Irish; the remarks of one honest Nationalist about another honest Nationalist. Similarly, while they are fond of poetry, they are not always fond of poets, and there is plenty of satire in their conversation on the subject. I have said that half the talk may consist of poetry; I might almost say that the other half may consist of parody. All these things amount to an excess of vigilance and realism; the mass of the people watch and pray, but even those who never pray never cease to watch. If they idealize sleep, it is as the sleepless do; it might almost be said that they can only dream of dreaming. If a dream haunts them, it is rather as something that escapes them; and indeed some of their finest poetry is rather about seeking fairyland than about finding it. Granted all this, I may say that there was one place in

Ireland where I did seem to find it, and not merely to seek it. There was one spot where I seemed to see the dream in possession, as one might see from afar a cloud resting on a single hill. There a dream, at once a desire and a delusion, brooded above a whole city. That place was Belfast.

The description could be justified even literally and in detail. A man told me in north-east Ulster that he had heard a mother warning her children away from some pond, or similar place of danger, by saying, "Don't you go there; there are wee popes there." A country where that could be said is like Elfland as compared to England. If not exactly a land of fairies, it is at least a land of goblins. There is something charming in the fancy of a pool full of these peculiar elves, like so many efts,[132] each with his tiny triple crown or crossed keys complete. That is the difference between this manufacturing district and an English manufacturing district, like that of Manchester. There are numbers of sturdy Nonconformists in Manchester, and doubtless they direct some of their educational warnings against the system represented by the Archbishop of Canterbury. But nobody in Manchester, however Nonconformist, tells even a child that a puddle is a sort of breeding place for Archbishops of Canterbury, little goblins in gaiters and aprons. It may be said that it is a very stagnant pool that breeds that sort of efts. But whatever view we take of it, it remains true, to begin with, that the paradox could be proved merely from superficial things like superstitions. Protestant Ulster reeks of superstition; it is the strong smell that really comes like a blast out of Belfast, as distinct from Birmingham or Brixton. But to me there is always something human and almost humanizing about superstition; and I really think that such lingering legends about the Pope, as a being as distant and dehumanised as the King of the Cannibal Islands, have served as a sort of negative folklore. And the same may be said, insofar as it is true that the commercial province has retained a theology as well as a mythology. Wherever men are still theological there is still some chance of their being logical. And in this the Calvinist Ulsterman may be more of a Catholic Irishman than is commonly realized, especially by himself.

Attacks and apologies abound about the matter of Belfast bigotry; but bigotry is by no means the worst thing in Belfast. I rather think it is the best. Nor is it the strongest example of what I mean, when I say that Belfast does really live in a dream. The other and more remarkable fault of the society has indeed a religious root; for nearly everything in history has a religious root, and especially nearly everything in Irish history. Of that theoretical origin in theology I may say something in a moment; it will be enough to say here that what has produced the more prominent and practical evil is ultimately the theology itself, but not the habit of being theological. It is the creed, but not the faith. Insofar as the Ulster Protestant really has a faith, he is really a fine fellow; though perhaps not quite so fine a fellow as he thinks himself. And that is the chasm; and can be most shortly stated as I have often stated it in such debates: by saying that the Protestant generally says, "I am a good Protestant," while the Catholic always says, "I am a bad Catholic."

When I say that Belfast is dominated by a dream, I mean it in the strict psychological sense; that something inside the mind is stronger than everything outside it. Nonsense is not only stronger than sense, but stronger than the senses. The idea in a man's head can eclipse the eyes in his head. Very worthy and kindly merchants told me there was no poverty in Belfast. They did not say there was less poverty than was commonly alleged, or less poverty than there had been, or less than there was in similar places elsewhere. They said there was none. As a remark about the Earthly Paradise or the New Jerusalem, it would be arresting. As a remark about the streets, through which they and I had both passed a few moments before, it was simply a triumph of the sheer madness of the imagination of man. These eminent citizens of Belfast received me in the kindest and most courteous fashion, and I would not willingly say anything in criticism of them beyond what is necessary for the practical needs of their country and mine. But indeed I think the greatest criticism on them, is that they would not understand what the criticism means. I will therefore clothe it in a parable, which is none the worse for having also been a real incident. When told there was no poverty in Belfast, I had remarked mildly that the people must have a singular taste in dress. I was gravely assured that they had indeed a most singular taste in dress. I was left with the general impression that wearing shirts or trousers decorated with large holes at irregular intervals was a pardonable form of foppery or fashionable extravagance. And it will always be a deep indwelling delight, in the memories of my life, that just as these city fathers and I came out on to the steps of the hotel, there appeared before us one of the raggedest of the ragged little boys I had seen, asking for a penny. I gave him a penny, whereon this group of merchants was suddenly transfigured into a sort of mob, vociferating, "Against the law! Against the law!" and bundled him away. I hope it is not unamiable to be so much entertained by that vision of a mob of magistrates, so earnestly shooing away a solitary child like a cat. Anyhow, they knew not what they did; and, what is worse, knew not what they knew not. And they would not understand, if I told them, what legend might have been made about that child, in the Christian ages of the world.

The point is here that the evil in the delusion does not consist in bigotry, but in vanity. It is not that such a Belfast man thinks he is right; for any honest man has a right to think he is right. It is that he does think he is good, not to say great; and no honest man can reach that comfortable conviction without a course of intellectual dishonesty. What cuts this spirit off from Christian common sense is the fact that the delusion, like most insane delusions, is merely egotistical. It is simply the pleasure of thinking extravagantly well of oneself, and unlimited indulgence in that pleasure is far more weakening than any indulgence in drink or dissipation. But so completely does it construct an unreal cosmos round the ego, that the criticism of the world cannot be felt even for worldly purposes. I could give many examples of this element in Belfast, as compared even with Birmingham and Manchester. The Lord Mayor of Manchester may not happen to know much about pictures, but he knows men who know about them. But the Belfast authorities will exhibit a maniacally bad picture as a masterpiece, merely because it glorifies Belfast. No man dare put up such a picture in Manchester, within a stone's throw of Mr. Charles Rowley.[133] I care comparatively little about the case of aesthetics; but the case is even clearer in ethics. So wholly are these people sundered from more Christian traditions that their very boasts lower them; and they abase themselves when they mean to exalt themselves. It never occurs to them that their strange inside standards do not always impress outsiders. A great employer introduced me to several of his very intelligent employees, and I can readily bear witness to the sincerity of the great Belfast delusion even among many of the poorer men of Belfast. But the sincere efforts of them and their master, to convince me that a union with the Catholic majority under Home Rule was intolerable to them, all went to one tune, which recurred with a kind of chorus, "We won't have the likes of them making laws for the likes of us." It never seemed to cross their minds that this is not a high example of any human morality; that judged by pagan *verecundia*[134] or Christian humility or modern democratic brotherhood, it is simply the remark of a snob. The man in question is quite innocent of all this; he has no notion of modesty, or even of mock modesty. He is not only superior, but he thinks it a superiority to claim superiority.

It is here that we cannot avoid theology, because we cannot avoid theory. For the point is that even in theory the one religious atmosphere now differs from the other. That the difference had historically a religious root is really unquestionable; but anyhow it is very deeply rooted. The essence of Calvinism was certainty about salvation; the essence of Catholicism is uncertainty about salvation. The modern and materialized form of that certainty is superiority; the belief of a man in a fixed moral aristocracy of men like himself. But the truth concerned here is that, by this time at any rate, the superiority has become a doctrine as well as an indulgence. I doubt if this extreme school of Protestants believe in Christian humility even as an ideal. I doubt whether the more honest of them would even profess to believe in it. This can be clearly seen by comparing it with other Christian virtues, of which this decayed Calvinism offers at least a version, even to those who think it a perversion. Puritanism is a version of purity; if we think it a parody of purity. Philanthropy is a version of charity; if we think it a parody of charity. But in all this commercial Protestantism there is no version of humility; there is not even a parody of humility. Humility is not an ideal. Humility is not even a hypocrisy. There is no institution, no commandment, no common form of words, no popular pattern or traditional tale, to tell anybody in any fashion that there is any such thing as a peril of spiritual pride. In short, there is here a school of thought and sentiment that does definitely regard self-satisfaction as a strength, as against the strong Christian tradition in the rest of the country that does as definitely regard it as a weakness. That is the real moral issue in the modern struggle in Ireland, nor is it confined to Ireland. England has been deeply infected with this pharisaical weakness, but as I have said, England takes things vaguely where Ireland takes them vividly. The men of Belfast offer that city as something supreme, unique and unrivalled; and they are very nearly right. There is nothing exactly like it in the industrialism of this country; but for all that, the fight against its religion of arrogance has been fought out elsewhere and on a larger field. There is another centre and citadel from which this theory, of strength in a self-hypnotized superiority, has despised Christendom. There has been a rival city to Belfast; and its name was Berlin.

Historians of all religions and no religion, may yet come to regard it as an historical fact, I fancy, that the Protestant Reformation of the sixteenth century (at least in the form it actually took) was a barbaric breakdown, like that Prussianism which was the ultimate product of that Protestantism. But however this may be, historians will always be interested to note that it produced certain curious and characteristic things, which are worth studying whether we like or dislike them. And one of its features, I fancy, has been this; that it has had the power of producing certain institutions which progressed very rapidly to great wealth and power; which the world regarded at a certain moment as invincible; and which the world, at the next moment, suddenly discovered to be intolerable. It was so with the whole of that Calvinist theology, of which Belfast is now left as the lonely missionary. It was so, even in our own time, with the whole of that industrial Capitalism of which Belfast is now the besieged and almost deserted outpost. And it was so with Berlin as it was with Belfast; and a subtle Prussian might almost complain of a kind of treachery, in the abruptness with which the world woke up and found it wanting; in the suddenness of the reaction that struck it impotent, so soon after it had been counted as omnipotent. These things seem to hold all the future, and in one flash they are things of the past.

Belfast is an antiquated novelty. Such a thing is still being excused for seeming *parvenu* when it is discovered to be *passé*. For instance, it is only by coming in touch with some of the controversies surrounding the Convention,[135] that an Englishman could realize how much the mentality of the Belfast leader is not so much that of a remote seventeenth century Whig, as that of a recent nineteenth century Radical. His conventionality seemed to be that of a Victorian rather than a Williamite, and to be less limited by the Orange Brotherhood[136] than by the Cobden Club.[137] This is a fact most successfully painted and pasted over by the big brushes of our own Party System, which has the art of hiding so many glaring facts. This Unionist Party in Ireland is very largely concerned to resist the main reform advocated by the Unionist Party in England. A political humorist, who understood the Cobden tradition of Belfast[138] and the Chamberlain traditiona of Birmingham,[139] could have a huge amount of fun appealing from one to the other; congratulating Belfast on the bold Protectionist doctrines prevalent in Ireland; abjuring Mr. Bonar Law and the Tariff Reformers[140] never to forget the fight made by Belfast for the sacred principles of Free Trade. But the fact that the Belfast school is merely the Manchester school is only one aspect of this general truth about the abrupt collapse into antiquity: a sudden superannuation. The whole march of that Manchester industrialism is not only halted but turned; the whole position is outflanked by new forces coming from new directions; the wealth of the peasantries blocks the road in front of it; the general strike has risen menacing its rear. That strange cloud of self-protecting vanity may still permit Belfast to believe in Belfast, but Britain does not really believe in Belfast. Philosophical forces far wider and deeper than politics have undermined the conception of progressive Protestantism in Ireland. I should say myself that mere English ascendancy in that island became intellectually impossible on the day when Shaftesbury introduced the first Factory Act, and on the day when Newman published the first pages of the *Apologia*. Both men were certainly Tories and probably Unionists. Neither were connected with the subject or with each other; the one hated the Pope and the other the Liberator. But industrialism was never again self-evidently superior after the first event, or Protestantism self-evidently superior after the second. And it needed a towering and self-evident superiority to excuse the English rule in Ireland. It is only on the ground of unquestionably doing good that men can do so much evil as that.

Some Orangemen before the war indulged in a fine rhetorical comparison between William of Prussia and William of Orange, and openly suggested that the new Protestant Deliverer from the north would come from North Germany. I was assured by my more moderate hosts in Belfast that such Orangemen could not be regarded as representative or even responsible. On that I cannot pronounce. The Orangemen may not have been representative; they may not have been responsible; but I am quite sure they were right. I am quite sure those poor fanatics were far nearer the nerve of historical truth than professional politicians like Sir Edward Carson or industrial capitalists like Sir George Clark.[141] If ever there was a natural alliance in the world, it would have been the alliance between Belfast and Berlin. The fanatics may be fools, but they have here the light by which the foolish things can confound the wise. It is the brightest spot in Belfast, bigotry, for if the light in its body be darkness, it is still brighter than the darkness. By the vision that goes everywhere with the virility and greatness of religion, these men had indeed pierced to the Protestant secret and meaning of four hundred years. Their Protestantism is Prussianism, not as a term of abuse, but as a term of abstract and impartial ethical science. Belfast and Berlin are on the same side in the deepest of all the spiritual issues involved in the war. And that is the simple issue of whether pride is a sin, and therefore a weakness. The modern mentality, or great masses of it, has seriously advanced the view that it is a weakness to disarm criticism by self-criticism, and a strength to disdain criticism through self-confidence. That is the thesis for which Berlin gave battle to the older civilization in Europe; and that for which Belfast gave battle to the older civilization in Ireland. It may be, as I suggested that such Protestant pride is the old Calvinism, with its fixed election of the few. It may be that the Protestantism is merely Paganism, with its brutish gods and giants lingering in corners of the more savage north. It may be that the Calvinism was itself a recurrence of the Paganism. But in any case, I am sure that this superiority, which can master men like a nightmare, can also vanish like a nightmare. And I strongly suspect that in this matter also, as in the matter of property as viewed by a peasantry, the older civilization will prove to be the real civilization, and that a healthier society will return to regarding pride as a pestilence, as the Socialists have already returned to regarding avarice as a pestilence. The old tradition of Christendom was that the highest form of faith was doubt. It was the doubt of a man about his soul. It was admirably expressed to me by Mr. Yeats, who is no champion of Catholic orthodoxy, in stating his preference for medieval Catholicism as compared with modern humanitarianism: "Men were thinking then about their own sins, and now they are always thinking about other peoples." And even by the Protestant test of progress, pride is seen to be arrested by a premature paralysis. Progress is superiority to oneself, and it is stopped dead by superiority to others. The case is even clearer by the test of poetry, which is much more solid and permanent than progress. The Superman may have been a sort of poem, but he could never be any sort of poet. The more we attempt to analyse that strange element of wonder, which is the soul of all the arts, the more we shall see that it must depend on some subordination of the self to a glory existing beyond it, and even in spite of it. Man always feels as a creature when he acts as a creator. When he carves a cathedral, it is to make a monster that can swallow him. But the Nietzschean nightmare of swallowing the world is only a sort of yawning. When the evolutionary anarch has broken all links and laws and is at last free to speak, he finds he has nothing to say. So German songs under the imperial eagle fell silent like songbirds under a hawk; and it is but rarely, and here and there, that a Belfast merchant liberates his soul in a lyric. He has to get Mr. Kipling[142] to write a Belfast poem, in a style technically attuned to the Belfast pictures. There is the true Tara of the silent harp, and the throne and habitation of the dream; and it is there that the Celtic pessimists should weep in silence for the end of the song. Blowing one's own trumpet has not proved a good musical education.

In logic a wise man will always put the cart before the horse. That is to say, he will always put the end before the means; when he is considering the question as a whole. He does not construct a cart in order to exercise a horse. He employs a horse to draw a cart, and whatever is in the cart. In all modern reasoning there is a tendency to make the mere political beast of burden more important than the chariot of man it is meant to draw. This has led to a dismissal of all such spiritual questions in favour of what are called social questions; and this is a too facile treatment of things like the religious question in Belfast. There is a religious question; and it will not have an irreligious answer. It will not be met by the limitation of Christian faith, but rather by the extension of Christian charity. But if a man says that there is no difference between a Protestant and a Catholic, and that both can act in an identical fashion everywhere but in a church or chapel, he is madly driving the cart horse when he has forgotten the cart. A religion is not the church a man goes to but the cosmos he lives in; and if any sceptic forgets it, the maddest fanatic beating an Orange drum about the Battle of the Boyne is a better philosopher than he.

Many uneducated and some educated people in Belfast quite sincerely believe that Roman priests are fiends, only waiting to rekindle the fires of the Inquisition. For two simple reasons, however, I declined to take this fact as evidence of anything except their sincerity. First, because the stories, when reduced to their rudiment of truth, generally resolved themselves into the riddle of poor Roman Catholics giving money to their own religion, and seemed to deplore not so much a dependence on priests as an independence of employers. And second, for a reason drawn from my own experience, as well as common knowledge, concerning the Protestant gentry in the south of Ireland. The southern Unionists spoke quite without this special horror of Catholic priests or peasants. They grumbled at them or laughed at them as a man grumbles or laughs at his neighbours; but obviously they no more dreamed that the priest would burn them than that he would eat them. If the priests were as black as the black Protestants painted them, they would be at their worst where they are with the majority, and would be known at their worst by the minority. It was clear that Belfast held the more bigoted tradition, not because it knew more of priests, but because it knew less of them; not because it was on the spot, but because the spot was barred. An even more general delusion was the idea that all the southern Irish dreamed and did no work. I pointed out that this also was inconsistent with concrete experience; since all over the world a man who makes a small farm pay has to work very hard indeed. In historic fact, the old notion that the Irish peasant did no work, but only dreamed, had a simple explanation. It merely meant that he did no work for a capitalist's profit, but dreamed of some day doing work for his own profit. But there may also have been this distorted truth in the tradition; that a free peasant, while he extends his own work, creates his own holidays. He is not idle all day, but he may be idle at any time of the day; he does not dream whenever he feels inclined, but he does dream whenever he chooses. A famous Belfast manufacturer, a man of capacity, but one who shook his head over the unaccountable prevalence of priests, assured me that he had seen peasants in the south doing nothing, at all sorts of odd times; and this is doubtless the difference between the farm and the factory. The same gentleman showed me over the colossal shipping of the great harbour, with all machinery and transport leading up to it. No man of any imagination would be insensible to such titanic experiments of his race; or deny the dark poetry of those furnaces fit for Vulcan or those hammers worthy of Thor. But as I stood on the dock I said to my guide: "Have you ever asked what all this is for?" He was an intelligent man, an exile from metaphysical Scotland, and he knew what I meant. "I don't know," he said, "perhaps we are only insects building a coral reef. I don't know what is the good of the coral reef." "Perhaps," I said, "that is what the peasant dreams about, and why he listens to the priest."

    For there seems to be a fashionable fallacy, to the effect that religious equality is something to be done and done with, that we may go on to the real matter of political equality. In philosophy it is the flat contrary that is true. Political equality is something to be done and done with, that we may go on to the much more real matter of religion. At the Abbey Theatre I saw a forcible play by Mr. St.

John Irvine,[143] called *The Mixed Marriage*, which I should remember if it were only for the beautiful acting of Miss Maire O'Neill.[144] But the play moved me very much as a play; yet I felt that the presence of this fallacy falsified it in some measure. The dramatist seemed to resent a schism merely because it interfered with a strike. But the only object of striking is liberty; and the only object of liberty is life: a thing wholly spiritual. It is economic liberty that should be dismissed as these people dismiss theology. We only get it to forget it. It is right that men should have houses, right that they should have land, right that they should have laws to protect the land; but all these things are only machinery to make leisure for the labouring soul. The house is only a stage set up by stage carpenters for the acting of what Mr. J. B. Yeats has called "the drama of the home." All the most dramatic things happen at home, from being born to being dead. What a man thinks about these things is his life; and to substitute for them a bustle of electioneering and legislation is to wander about among screens and pulleys on the wrong side of pasteboard scenery, and never to act the play. And that play is always a miracle play; and the name of its hero is Everyman.

When I came back from the desolate splendour of the Donegal sea and shore, and saw again the square garden and the statue outside the Dublin hotel, I did not know I was returning to something that might well be called more desolate. For it was when I entered the hotel that I first found that it was full of the awful tragedy of the Leinster.[145] I had often seen death in a home, but never death decimating a vast hostelry; and there was something strangely shocking about the empty seats of men and women with whom I had talked so idly a few days before. It was almost as if there was more tragedy in the cutting short of such trivial talk than in the sundering of life-long ties. But there was all the dignity as well as the tragedy of man; and I was glad, before I left Ireland, to have seen the nobler side of the Anglo-Irish garrison, and to have known men of my own blood, however mistaken, so enduring the end of things. With the bad news from the sea came better news from the war; the Teutonic hordes were yielding everywhere, at the signal of the last advance; and with all the emotions of an exile, however temporary, I knew that my own land was secure. Somehow, the bad and good news together turned my mind more and more towards England;

and all the inner humour and insular geniality which even the Irish may some day be allowed to understand. As I went homewards on the next boat that started from the Irish port, and the Wicklow hills receded in a rainy and broken sunlight, it was with all the simplest of those ancient appetites with which a man should come back to his own country. Only there clung to me, not to be denied, one sentiment about Ireland, one sentiment that I could not transfer to England; which called me like an elfland of so many happy figures, from Puck to Pickwick.[146] As I looked at those rainy hills I knew at least that I was looking, perhaps for the last time, on something rooted in the Christian faith. There at least the Christian ideal was something more than an ideal; it was in a special sense real. It was so real that it appeared even in statistics. It was so self-evident as to be seen even by sociologists. It was a land where our religion had made even its vision visible. It had made even its unpopular virtues popular. It must be, in the times to come, a final testing-place, of whether a people that will take that name seriously, and even solidly, is fated to suffer or to succeed.

As the long line of the mountain coast unfolded before me I had an optical illusion; it may be that many have had it before. As new lengths of coast and lines of heights were unfolded, I had the fancy that the whole land was not receding but advancing, like something spreading out its arms to the world. A chance shred of sunshine rested, like a riven banner, on the hill which I believe is called in Irish the Mountain of the Golden Spears; and I could have imagined that the spears and the banner were coming on. And in that flash I remembered that the men of this island had once gone forth, not with the torches of conquerors or destroyers, but as missionaries in the very midnight of the Dark Ages; like a multitude of moving candles, that were the light of the world.

Notes.

[1] St. Stephen. First Christian martyr, stoned to death by members of the Synagogue after being falsely accused of blasphemy and brought before the Sanhedrin, a scene recounted in the Acts of the Apostles, Chapter vii.

[2] From the second verse of the poem/song, "The Wearing of the Green," by Dion Boucicault (1820–1890). In spite of his French surname, he was a Dublin-born Irishman; later became famous in America for the song, "A Bicycle Built for Two."

[3] James Clarence Mangan (1803–1849). Regarded as the leading Anglo-Irish poet of the nineteenth century. Personally a social disaster, who was addicted to alcohol and drugs and died of cholera. Nonetheless, he wrote a number of celebrated poems, including "Ode to the Maguire," "Farewell to Patrick Sarsfield," and "The Lament for the Princes of Tyrone and Tyrconnell."

[4] Cubism. A style of art – especially in painting – in which objects are so presented as to give the effect of an assemblage of geometrical figures. The movement existed between 1907 and 1914 and was developed by Pablo Picasso (1882–1973) and George Braque (1882–1963). It came into existence after the artist Paul Cézanne suggested that nature be treated "in terms of the cylinder, the sphere and the cone." In *Miscellany of Men* Chesterton refers to it as one of "the latest artistic insanities."

[5] Vorticism. An early twentieth century English artistic and literary movement that had roots in Cubism and affinities to Futurism. It involved the poet Ezra Pound (1885–1972), the author Wyndham Lewis (1882–1957), and the sculptor Gaudier Brzeska (1891–1915). The principle achievement of the movement was the production of two numbers of its journal, *Blast*.

[6] Dublin Arts Club. One of several independent societies for the arts in Dublin, founded in 1886; quickly became a gathering place for artists, writers, and visionaries.

[7] Glorious Revolution and Protestant Deliverer. A reference to events in England in 1688–89 when a cabal of Parliamentary magnates – Howards, Russells and Cecils – overthrew the legitimate Stuart king, James II, because of his conversion to, and advocacy of, Catholicism (which threatened the ill-gotten gains of the aforementioned cabal) and placed in his stead the sodomite, William, Prince of Orange, referred to as the "Protestant Deliverer." From that point on, the history of England is but the story of unchecked Parliamentary control of the country, masquerading as "the will of the English people."

⁸ Hanoverian Succession. An important preoccupation of English politics from 1702 to 1707. The Hanoverian Succession would ensure that the successor to Queen Anne, who had no surviving issue of her own, would be a Protestant of the House of Hanover, and would hold the Scottish as well as the English Crowns. By Act of the English Parliament, the English Crown was already slated to succeed to the Protestant House of Hanover; it was ardently desired by the English that such would be the case for the Scottish Crown, to avoid the possibility that the Scottish Crown would pass to a Catholic Jacobite (*vide infra*). The English employed financial pressure, bribery, and polemic to force the Scottish Parliament to accept a treaty uniting the two nations in 1707, thus eliminating that latter possibility.

⁹ Whig. A member of the political party that, after the Revolution of 1688, aimed at subordinating (and successfully so) the power of the Crown to Parliament, which they controlled.

¹⁰ Hill of Tara. A low-lying ridge situated mid-way between Dunshaughlin and Navan in County Meath. It has been regarded traditionally as the seat of the High Kings of Ireland. The most renowned of many tales associated with Tara relates how, in his campaign to bring Catholicism to Ireland, St. Patrick lit the Paschal fire on the Hill of Slane and confronted Loegaire, King of Tara, and his druids.

¹¹ "Tararaboomdeay." A trivial song made famous by dancer/singer, Lottie Collins (1865–1910).

¹² Home Rule. A proposal put on the table by the British government a number of times during the late nineteenth and early twentieth century, whereby the Irish would be a given a Parliament with various degrees of authority but which would always be subservient to the Imperial Parliament in London. It was frequently suggested in order to assuage rising Irish nationalist and Irish Republican sentiment, but when it was finally made law during World War I, it was immediately suspended pending the end of the war. Thereafter Dominion Home Rule was never taken seriously by Irish public opinion.

¹³ Unionism. As a political tradition, it can be traced back to that strand of late seventeenth and early eighteenth century "patriotism" which held that full political integration with Great Britain was preferable to a flawed or unattainable legislative independence. When the Act of Union was forced upon Ireland in 1801, Unionism still lacked a popular base. The first formal Irish Unionist organization came into being in 1885–86 when the Home Rule crisis of the day provoked this as a reaction. Since then Unionism has principally centered in the North-east corner of Ireland, and is largely identified with the Protestant community.

¹⁴ Karl Marx (1818–1883). German-born Jewish economic and political philosopher. Went to Paris, France in 1843 where he met his companion and friend for life, Friedrich Engels – and between them developed the theory and tactics of the creed that became known as Communism. Both joined the secretive Communist League in 1847 and at the insistence of the League's leaders wrote the now infamous *Communist Manifesto*. Marx moved to London in 1849 where he wrote his most important work, *Das Kapital*, the first volume of which was published in 1867.

¹⁵ Manchester School. A term first used by the nineteenth century British politician, Benjamin Disraeli, and which referred to the movement in favour of "free trade" in England. The School's roots were to be found in the Manchester-based Anti-Corn Law League of Richard Cobden (1804–1865) and John Bright (1811–1889). Since that time, the meaning of the term has widened so as to encompass libertarianism in economic policy, radical liberalism in politics, and unfettered "free trade." Thus the contemporary meaning is both economic and political.

¹⁶ William Morris (1834–1896). English artist, author, journalist, and social activist. A chief Victorian-era critic of Industrialism, he was an eclectic Socialist who was also variously influenced by the High Anglican "Oxford Movement" of Newman, Keble and Pusey, and the legacy of medieval life and art. In 1856, he embarked on an artistic career, becoming famous for his poetry, his wallpapers, his designs, his writings and his typography; he became the chief inspiration behind the Arts and Crafts movement (1870–1900) which desired to elevate the applied arts to the status of fine arts, and to restore a human scale and dimension to production of useful goods. His critique of Industrialism led him to embrace Socialism; in 1884 he founded the Socialist League, and for a time was editor of its journal, *Commonweal*. Refused the Poet Laureateship in 1891, following Tennyson's death.

¹⁷ George Wyndham (1863–1913). A scion of the English aristocracy which claimed descent from the rebel Lord Edward Fitzgerald. A liberal Tory, Wyndham was Chief Secretary for Ireland from 1900–1905. An ambitious reformer, he is best remembered in Ireland for his success in putting the Land Act of 1903 on the books, whereby Irish tenants could buy out the owners steadily and piecemeal. It was an action that allowed much of the land confiscated from the Irish by the English to pass back into Irish hands.

¹⁸ Horace Plunkett (1854–1932). A member of the Anglo-Irish nobility, Horace Plunkett was the pioneer of agricultural co-operation in Ireland.

He launched the Co-operative Movement in 1889, having spent the previous 10 years ranching in Wyoming, USA. Elected a Liberal Unionist MP in 1892, he proved that he was wholly indifferent as a politician. His best known work, *Ireland in the New Century* (1904), caused grave offence because of his claim that the influence of the Catholic Church was "baleful."

[19] John Russell (1792–1878). The son of the Duke of Bedford, entered Parliament in 1813. Involved in the drafting of the 1832 Reform Bill which greatly expanded the franchise in England. Prime Minister from 1846–1852, and made a Lord in 1861. His memory is reviled in Ireland because it is believed that his rigid adherence to the so-called iron laws of Political Economy led to the unnecessary deaths of many thousands of Irish during the Irish Famine of the 1840s.

[20] Coercion Acts. A general term for a series of measures commencing with the Suppression of Disturbance Act (1833), which empowered the Lord Lieutenant to proclaim a district as disturbed, thereby permitting the imposition of a curfew and other restrictions. It also provided for trial by military courts rather than by magistrates in special session. Other Acts appeared in 1847, 1856, 1871, 1881, 1882 and 1887, all of which sought to suppress "subversive activity" by increasing restrictive police and legal powers.

[21] Land Acts. A term to cover a series of Acts implemented over a period of roughly 50 years. The Landlord and Tenant (Ireland) Act (1870) gave force of law to customary tenant right where it existed, and created it in other parts of the country. It was followed by the Land Law (Ireland) Act (1881), the Purchase of Land (Ireland) Act (1885), the Balfour Act (1891), and the Wyndham Act (1903) (*vide supra*). Collectively, they transformed land-holding in Ireland from landlordism to owner occupation.

[22] Caporetto. A reference to the military offensive launched in early October, 1917, by German and Austrian divisions, against Caporetto on the Isonzo Front which was lightly defended by the Italian Army. By October 24, General Luigi Cadorna gave the Italians orders to retreat, having lost over 300,000 men and most of their trench artillery.

[23] Alexander Kerensky (1881–1970). Trained as a lawyer and then entered the Russian Socialist Revolutionary Party in 1905, becoming the editor of its radical paper, *Burevestik*. Elected to the State Duma in 1912, having won much popularity from the working classes for his defence of "subversives." Member of a Provisional government headed by Prince George Lvov, set up following the abdication of Czar Nicholas II; became head of the government on July 8, 1917. After much in-fighting among both members of

the government army and the Bolsheviks, he was ousted and went into exile. He spent from 1939 until his death at the Hoover Institute in America.

[24] General Lavr Kornilov (1870–1918). Graduated from the Mikhailovsky Artillery Training Corps in 1892. After the Czar's abdication, he became Commander in Chief of the Petrograd Garrison, and Supreme Commander of the Russian Army under Minister of War, Kerensky. He tried to arrest the Revolution in 1917 by attacking Petrograd, but at Kerensky's request the Bolsheviks stopped him. Kornilov became one of the commanders of the White Army during the Civil War (1918–1921), and died in action.

[25] George Russell (1867–1935). Irish author who often wrote under the pseudonym "A.E." An active Irish nationalist, editor of *Irish Homestead* from 1904 to 1923, and of the *Irish Statesman* from 1923 to 1930. He is regarded as one of the greatest writers of the Irish Literary revival.

[26] *Le Roi le veult*. "The King so wishes it."

[27] Charles Stuart Parnell (1846–1891). Protestant landlord who entered Parliament in 1875 and joined the Home Rule party. In 1879, he became President of Michael Davitt's Irish National Land League – which sought peasant proprietorship, and was leader of the Irish Parliamentary Party from 1880, becoming, thereby, the "uncrowned King of Ireland." In 1885, Parnell's Irish Parliamentary Party won a landslide victory, but his involvement with Mrs. O'Shea in a messy divorce case split the Party ca. 1890 and he died soon after.

[28] Fenianism. A revolutionary movement that originated amongst the Irish emigrants to the USA following the collapse of the Young Ireland movement and the discrediting of Parliamentary agitation. Fenianism sought the creation of an independent Irish Republic. The men chiefly responsible for the setting up of the Fenian movement were John O'Mahony (1816–1877), Michael Doheny (1805–1863), and James Stephens (1824–1901). Sinn Fein was a politically nationalist group founded and led by Arthur Griffith (1871–1922). Contrary to popular belief, Sinn Fein played no part in the 1916 Rebellion (also called the "Easter Rising"), though the British insisted on calling the rebels "Shinners."

[29] Fr. Bernard Vaughan (1847–1922). A prominent late nineteenth and early twentieth century Jesuit preacher, who worked in Manchester and at famous Farm St. mission in London. Brother of Cardinal Herbert Vaughan. The dedication of his book, *Society, Sin and the Saviour* (1907), read: "To you my brothers and sisters, who like Annas, Caiphas, Pilate and Herod are vainly striving to rid yourselves and your country of Jesus Christ."

[30] Arnold Bennett (1867–1931). An English journalist and associate of the Fabian Society. Directed the *New Statesman*, journal of the Fabian Society, for a time before his death.

Irish Impressions   131

[31] Probably a reference to the author of *The Destitute Alien: A Series of Essays dealing with the subject of Foreign Pauper Immigration*, published in 1892. He was concerned with the flood of immigration into the Britain of his day, and particularly with the influx of Russian and Polish Jews into the East End of London.

[32] Probably a reference to the author of *Happy India: and How it Might be Guided by Modern Science*, published in 1922, which argued, against William Digby who blamed British Imperial policy, that the roots of India's poverty and misery lay in Hinduism and the apathy of the higher castes.

[33] Prof. Gilbert Murray (1866–1957). Regius Professor of Greek at Oxford University, England. Wrote *The Five Stages of Greek Religion* and *The Interpretation of Greek Literature*. The most popular Hellenist of his age, he was, nonetheless, viciously attacked by T. S. Eliot for his work on Euripides. Eliot wrote: "It is because Murray has no creative instinct that he leaves Euripides quite dead."

[34] Sir Gilbert Parker (1862–1932). A Canadian writer whose novels and tales were heavily permeated with the history of Canada and with praise of the British Empire. His most popular works were *Pierre and His People* (1892), *The Seats of the Mighty* (1896) and *The Promised Land* (1928). He moved to England in 1889, and sat in the British Parliament from 1900 until 1918.

[35] Sir Edward Henry (1850–1931). Appointed Inspector General of Bengal Police in 1891, he became interested in the work of Galton and others who sought to use fingerprints as a method of identifying criminals. Between July 1896 and February 1897, he devised a system of classification for fingerprints which, within a short time, was adopted worldwide. He was appointed Commissioner of Scotland Yard – the headquarters of the British Police – in 1903, and was responsible for the founding of its Fingerprint Bureau.

[36] Edward Clodd (1840–1930). A rationalist and Darwinist writer, who was also the President of the Folklore Society. He believed that he could debunk religion through his advocacy of Evolution theory. He wrote *An Essay in Savage Philosophy in Folk Tale* (1898), *Pioneers of Evolution Theory from Thales to Huxley* (1907), and *Animism: Primitive Myth and Religion*(1921).

[37] William S. Porter (1862–1910). American author known for his short stories, written under the pseudonym "O. Henry."

[38] Sir John Barker (1840–1914). Wealthy owner of the Knightsbridge, London, emporium of the same name. A close friend of the Liberal politician, David Lloyd George.

[39] John Masefield (1878–1967). English writer who began as a journalist and whose first volume, *Salt Water Ballads*, was published in 1902. Wrote

Gallipoli, which was published in 1916, and covered the disastrous campaign of WWI. His autobiography, *In the Mill*, was published in 1941. Became Poet Laureate in 1930 and remained so until his death.

[40] Harley Granville Barker (1877–1946). English actor, producer, director and dramatist. Renowned for his Shakespearean productions, he also produced his own plays, which included *The Voysey Inheritance* (1905) and *The Madras House* (1910). After WWI, he became President of the British Drama League. He began writing his now famous work, *Prefaces to Shakespeare* in 1923, which was published between 1927 and 1948.

[41] A central south-western district of London, England.

[42] *Daily Mail*. Daily newspaper founded by Alfred Harmsworth, Lord Northcliffe (1865–1922), in 1894; still one of the major British tabloids.

[43] Sir Edward Henry Carson, Lord of Duncairn (1854–1935). Protestant lawyer who became MP for Trinity College, Dublin in 1892. Solicitor General for Ireland (1892) and England (1900-1905); Attorney General for Great Britian (1915–1916) in Herbert Asquith's government. Violently hostile to Irish Home Rule, he became leader of the Irish Unionist Parliamentary Party in 1910, supported the paramilitary gun-running efforts of the Ulster Volunteer Force, and was in favor of the Partition of Ireland.

[44] James Henry Mussen Campbell, Lord Glenavy (1851 - 1931). Barrister and Irish Unionist MP from St. Stephen's Green (1898–1900) and University of Dublin (1903–1916); colleague of Carson, who was also MP from the University (1892–1918). Member of provisional government of Ireland, formed by Carson as an element of his anti-Home Rule agitation. Lord Chief Justice of Ireland, 1916–1918.

[45] *Morning Post*. Daily newspaper founded in 1772. Initially employed notable writers such as Samuel Coleridge, Robert Southey, William Wordsworth and Charles Lamb to improve its status and circulation. Purchased by Sir James Berry, owner of the *Daily Telegraph*, a paper founded in 1855, and still being published; contrary to Berry's original intentions, the two papers were quickly amalgamated.

[46] *Saturday Review*. London weekly newspaper founded in 1855 to combat the influence of *The Times*. Ceased publication ca. 1938.

[47] Jacobite. Supporter of James II and his son James Stuart, "the Old Pretender," and of their right to the English throne. Support was based largely in Scotland and Ireland. There were several revolts in their favor, but the Stuart army, under Bonne Prince Charlie, was eventually annihilated at Culloden, Scotland in 1745. Not to be confused with the "Jacobins" of the French Revolution.

Irish Impressions 133

[48] Williamite. Supporter of William III, of the House of Orange, in his war against the legitimate Stuart King, James II, between 1689–91.

[49] F. E. Smith, Lord Birkenhead (1872–1930). Educated at Oxford University and elected as a Conservative MP in 1906. A brilliant orator. He was violently anti-Home Rule for Ireland, though ironically he got on very well with Michael Collins, the leader of the Irish War of Independence which culminated in the Treaty founding the Irish Free State in 1922. He was granted his lordship in 1919 by Lloyd George, and was Lord Chancellor of England from 1919 to 1922.

[50] Sir Roger Casement (1864–1916). Joined the British Colonial Service in 1892, and established an international reputation for his reporting of the terrible exploitation of native workers in Africa and Hispanic America by European employers. Knighted in 1911, he retired two years later. A founding member of the Irish Volunteers, he believed passionately that for an Irish uprising to succeed, it needed German help. He obtained wholly inadequate support and returned to Ireland to propose the postponing of the Rebellion. Arrested on the Banna Strand, he was executed in August 1916. Converted to Catholicism shortly before his hanging.

[51] Robert Browning (1812–1889). English poet who married the celebrated poet, Elizabeth Barrett. His best collection of poetry is generally held to be *Men and Women*, though it was *The Ring and the Book*, published in 1868 and 1869, which brought him considerable popularity in his own lifetime. His final published volume was *Asolando*, which appeared on the day of his death.

[52] Andrew Kettle (1833-1916). Irish farmer involved in the Irish Land Movement who presided at the first meeting of the National Land League in 1879. "Right hand man" to Charles Stuart Parnell (*vide supra*). Kettle's son, Thomas (1880–1916), was a poet and essayist, and a Nationalist MP for East Tyrone for four years. Was in Belgium purchasing weapons for the Irish Volunteers when WWI began; outraged by the German invasion, he switched his support to the Allies and died in action in France.

[53] William E. Gladstone (1809–1898). British Prime Minister four times between 1868 and 1894. Strongly Anglican in religion, he supported *laissez-faire* economics, but opposed Income Tax.

[54] Benjamin Disraeli (1804–1881). British politician who was variously a Conservative, a Whig, a Radical and an Independent. Helped form the *Young England* group in 1842 which advocated an alliance between the working classes and the aristocracy. This doctrine appeared in his novels *Coningsby* (1844), *Sybil* (1845) and *Tancred* (1847). He became Prime Minister in 1868.

⁵⁵ Factory Acts. A series of legislation in the United Kingdom in the nineteenth century which sought to protect workers – principally woman and children – from the appalling conditions of rampant Capitalism. The first was passed in 1802 and stipulated that children over 10 years of age could only work 12 hours a day. The Acts originally applied only to the cotton industry, but they were subsequently extended; 18 acts were passed between 1802 and 1891.

⁵⁶ A reference to the Battle of St. Quentin in France which took place between March 21 and March 23, 1918. It was part of the first phase of the First Battle of the Somme in 1918.

⁵⁷ Jim Larkin (1874–1947). Abrasive and rather dictatorial leader of the Irish Transport and General Workers Union, which he founded in 1909 after splitting with James Sexton of the National Union of Dock Labourers as a result of friction between them. Best remembered for his pivotal role in the 1913 Dublin Lockout which ended in failure.

⁵⁸ James Connolly (1868–1916). Irish labour leader born in Edinburgh, Scotland. Imbibed his Irish nationalism from a Fenian uncle and his Socialism from the extremely grim life of the working class of the day. Became the head of the Irish Transport and General Workers Union, when Jim Larkin went to America following the collapse of the 1913 Lockout. A prolific writer, his best known works are *Labour in Irish History* (1910) and *The Re-conquest of Ireland* (1915). Became the military commander of the Easter Rebellion in 1916, and was executed sometime after. Despite his socialist convictions, he died in communion with the Church.

⁵⁹ William Martin Murphy (1844–1919). A capitalist who was typical of the conservative ranks of the Irish Nationalist Party. He established the Dublin United Tramways Company, and bought two nationalist papers, *The Irish Catholic* and the *Irish Independent*. Founder of the Dublin Employers' Federation in 1912, he was active in combating the rising labour agitation, which culminated in the Dublin Lockout of 1913.

⁶⁰ *Et pour cause.* "And for a good reason."

⁶¹ Parsee. Member of a small community in India whose religion descends from the Persian adherents of the dualistic religion of Zoroastrianism; they fled to India in the seventh and eight centuries because of Muslim persecution. The doctrines of this religion are codified in the *Zend-Avesta*, and posit perpetual war between Ormuzd, the god of light, and Ahriman, the spirit of darkness.

⁶² Hugh Alexander Law (1872–1943). Irish Nationalist MP for Donegal in pre- and post- WWI Ireland.

[63] William Butler Yeats (1865–1939). The greatest of the Anglo-Irish poets. His first poems were published in the 1880s, but thereafter he drew extensively upon Gaelic literature and County Sligo folklore, the county of his birth. He was heavily involved in advanced nationalist circles, an activity which led to the founding of the Irish Literary Theatre – subsequently to be called the Abbey Theatre. Of Protestant ancestry, he was well-known for his opposition to Catholic clericalism and his support for the Irish Blue Shirt movement of the 1930s. Chesterton's reference is to his poem, "The Lake Isle of Innisfree":

> I will arise and go now, and go to Innisfree,
> And a small cabin build there, of clay and wattles made;
> Nine bean rows will I have there, a hive for the honey bee,
> And live alone in the bee-loud glade.

[64] Katherine Tynan (1868–1931). A well-known Irish authoress, who penned more than 100 novels.

[65] Stephen Gwynne (1864–1950). The Oxford educated, Protestant Nationalist MP for Galway from 1906–1918. He wrote extensively, producing biographies, historical works and literary criticism. He fought for the Allies in WWI.

[66] James Stephens (1824–1901). Took part in the abortive Irish rebellion of 1848, which led to his exile in Paris. Founded the Irish Republican Brotherhood in Dublin in 1858, becoming the nominal head of the Fenian movement in America in 1859. He established a successful propaganda paper, *Irish People*, and built himself a great popularity in the early 1860s. However in December 1866, he repudiated the rising that he had promised for the end of that year; as a result, his influence and popularity drained away. Died quietly in Dublin, shunned by subsequent IRB leaders and followers.

[67] Dr. Oliver St. John Gogarty (1878–1957). Obtained his Medical degree from Trinity College, Dublin, in 1907, though he had already acquired a reputation as a versatile controversialist and as a promising poet. A friend of James Joyce, he is said to have been the model for "Buck Mulligan" from Joyce's work, *Ulysses*. He served for a time in the Irish Senate, but was largely devoted to lecturing and writing. His *Collected Poems* were published in 1951, and the best known of his eight novels are *As I was Walking Down Sackville Street* (1937) and *It isn't That Time of Year at All* (1954).

[68] Walt Whitman (1819–1892). Well-known American poet, whose work celebrated freedom, democracy and the brotherhood of man. His *Leaves of Grass* was first published in 12 volumes in 1855 and by 1892 had expanded to over 300 volumes.

⁶⁹ Liberty Hall. The original building purchased in 1912 for the Irish Transport and General Workers Union under Jim Larkin. Situated on Eden Quay, Dublin, it was extensively damaged during the 1916 Rising. It remained in use until 1956 when it was demolished and replaced by the present 17-story HQ of the union.

⁷⁰ Thomas Johnson (1872–1963). Born in Liverpool, England; had various jobs that took him to Ireland. Became Vice President of the Irish Trades Union Congress in 1913, and President in 1916. He was actively involved in the anti-conscription campaign of 1918. He became the TD – equivalent of MP in Ireland – for County Dublin in 1922 and remained so for five years. He was the leader of the Parliamentary Labour Party until 1928.

⁷¹ Cf. 1 Kings 21: 1–29.

⁷² Probably a reference to Joseph Devlin (1871–1934). A working class Catholic from Belfast, he became one of the leading Ulster MP's of the Nationalist Party. He became the Chairman of the newspaper, *Irish News*, as well as President of the Ancient Order of Hibernians. In the post-1916 period, he sought to convince Northern nationalists to vote for temporary partition. His reputation never recovered from that error.

⁷³ Tim Healy (1855–1931). A well-known Irish politician renowned for his maverick tendencies, high income, and sharp tongue.

⁷⁴ *Delenda est....* In English, "...must be destroyed." From Cato's repeated statement "Carthage must be destroyed" (*"Delenda est Carthago"*), urging the Roman Senate to make war upon Carthage.

⁷⁵ Byzantium. The East Roman Empire.

⁷⁶ Crescent. The symbol of Islam.

⁷⁷ John Sobieski (1629–1692). A Polish warrior who rose to the position of Commander in Chief under King Casimir, and became a national hero when he wiped out the Turkish army at Chocimin in 1672. Elected King John III in 1674. When the Grand Vizier, Mustapha, appeared before the Gates of Vienna in 1683, with some 210,000 men, Sobieski was his principal opponent for Christendom. On September 12, Sobieski attacked with a mere 76,000 and crushed the Islamic army. He sent Pope Innocent XI the "Standard of the Prophet" captured from the Grand Vizier, and a letter in which he adapted Caesar's words to the occasion: "I came, I saw, God conquered." In the Islamic world, Sobieski was known as the "unvanquished Northern Lion."

⁷⁸ In 878 King Alfred the Great (849–899) of Anglo-Saxon England successfully defended Wessex from the Vikings.

⁷⁹ Battle of Marathon. Clash of September 490BC between Persians

under Darius I, who invaded the Greek mainland, and the Greeks under Miltiades, who, though outnumbered 4 to 1, destroyed the invading army. Roughly 6,400 Persians were killed; Athenian casualties were below 200. The Archons were the nine principle magistrates of ancient Athens.

[80] Attila (c406–453). King of the Huns from 433–453; probably of Mongol stock. The Huns appeared on the fringes of the Roman Empire from the Steppes of Asia, and won sweeping victories through their astute use of horse-born archers. Roman General Flavius Aetius (c396–454) was the first to defeat Attila at the Battle of Chalons in Gaul (451).

[81] William the Conqueror (1028–1087). Duke of Normandy whose kingdom was the most powerful vassal of the French Crown. Following the victory over the Anglo-Saxons in 1066, he was consecrated King of England in Westminster Abbey in 1067, though revolts broke out in Exeter, the Welsh Borders and Northumbria immediately afterwards. The revolts were suppressed violently. However, William greatly improved the condition of the Church in England.

[82] St. Thomas Aquinas (1225–1274). The official Philosopher of the Catholic Church. His first Summa was the *Summa of Christian Teaching*, which was prepared specifically to deal with those who did not have the Catholic faith: pagans, Jews, Greek schismatics, and Muslims. His second, begun in 1266, was the *Summa Theologica* for which he is most famous, and which was a beginner's (!) introduction to Catholic theology. Mary Clarke, the Thomist writer, says: "To know St. Thomas is to know the medieval mind at its finest, its most powerful, and, indeed, its most modern. For he is timeless and timely, a man for all ages."

[83] Charles Fox (1749–1806). A dissolute English politician who entered Parliament in 1768; supported the French Revolution and helped abolish the Slave Trade.

[84] Max Beerbohm (1872–1956). Critic, essayist and caricaturist. He was the Drama critic of the *Saturday Review* from 1898 to 1910, having succeeded George Bernard Shaw. His caricatures were collected in works such as *A Christmas Garland*, published in 1912. From 1935, he took to broadcasting. His major works include: *A.V. Laider, Rossetti and his Circle*, and *Zuleika Dobson*.

[85] RMS Lusitania. The "Queen of the Seas" was the pride of the Cunard Line and was launched in 1906; its maiden voyage took place in September, 1907, and it transported 3,000 passengers to New York. On May 1, 1915, it was requisitioned by the Royal Navy because of the needs of WWI, and so left New York en route for Liverpool. On May 7, 1915, the German U-

Boat 20 torpedoed it in the Irish Channel. Some 18 minutes later, despite its allegedly innovative construction in two parts, it sank with the loss of 1,195 lives. The controversy over its sinking is still raging, for although survivors are unanimous in saying that they heard two explosions, the U-Boat log of Captain Schweigen shows that only one torpedo was fired. The accusation remains that the Lusitania was illegally carrying high explosives to England, and that therefore the German government regarded it as a legitimate target.

[86] Walter Alison Phillips (1864–1950). Lecky Professor of Modern History at Trinity College, Dublin. Violently opposed to Home Rule, he declared that "Ireland is not a nation, but two peoples separated by a deeper gulf than that dividing Ireland from Great Britain." Chief assistant editor of the *Encyclopaedia Britannica* (11th edition). Also wrote a number of works of modern European history.

[87] Armenia. A region of Southwest Asia east of Turkey conquered frequently by numerous peoples – in many cases Islamic – including the Mongols, the Seljuk Turks, and the Ottoman Turks; in 1915 hundreds of thousands of Armenian Christians were massacred, though the whole subject remains disputed by the Turks.

[88] In Charles Dickens's novel, *The Pickwick Papers* (1836), a fictional Parliamentary election takes place in the town of Eatanswill between Messrs. Slumkey and Fizkin, representing the Blue and Buff parties respectively.

[89] Excerpt from the phrase "Kill them all! God will know His own" reputedly uttered by the Abbot Arnauld Amaury at the siege of Béziers in southern France, during the suppression of the Albigensian heresy in the twelfth century. The Catholics refused to leave the city stronghold of the Cathars; Amaury declared that since men could not distinguish the faithful from the heretic, it would be left to God – hence the famous quotation.

[90] Second Battle of the Marne. 1918 battle in World War I from which the allies emerged victorious, and which represented a significant turning point of the war in their favor. Marshal Ferdinand Foch (1851–1929), a strong Catholic, was acting as Allied Supreme Commander at the time; he was also Chief of the French General Staff from 1917.

[91] A reference to the Irish insurrection of 1798, which was the culmination of the revolutionary activities of the United Irishmen. There were four main outbreaks: risings in Counties Dublin, Kildare and Meath in April and May; in eastern Ulster in early June; in County Wexford in late May and early June; and on and off until 1803 in the province of Connacht. Overall the rebellion resulted in the death of some 30,000 people.

[92] Walter Hume Long (1854–1924). Elected a Conservative MP in 1880; became President of the Board of Agriculture in 1895. Chief Secretary of Ireland from 1905 to 1906. Became First Lord of the Admiralty in 1919, and was granted the title Viscount Long of Wraxall.

[93] David Lloyd George (1863–1946). Entered Parliament as a Liberal Member in 1890. Served in various government posts, notably as Chancellor of the Exchequer under Herbert Asquith from 1908 to 1915. Became Prime Minister in 1916 after striking a deal with Conservatives to oust Asquith; he remained in the post until his resignation in 1922. He continued to lead the Liberal party for a number of years.

[94] Young Ireland Movement. A romantic nationalist group active in the period 1842–48, led by Thomas Davis (1814–1845), Charles Gavan Duffy (1816–1903) and John Blake Dillon (1816–1866). It formed around the *Nation* newspaper, and was made up of middle class graduates from Trinity College, Dublin, from both Catholic and Protestant backgrounds. It sought to create a non-sectarian public opinion infused with a sense of cultural nationality; it believed that a national literature and the Irish language had to be promoted, though they did very little to implement such principles. Their support was largely restricted to Dublin, and they were not highly regarded by most Catholic clergy.

[95] A reference to Thomas Francis Meagher (1823–1867), a Young Irelander who became famous for his attacks on Daniel O'Connell's peace resolutions in 1846, a stance which earned him the nickname "Meagher of the Sword." He later became a journalist in New York and commanded the pro-Union Irish Brigade in the American Civil War. Drowned in Missouri in 1867.

[96] *Atalanta in Calydon: A Tragedy.* Published in 1865 by the poet Algernon Charles Swinburne (1837–1909).

[97] Kaffir. Member of a Bantu-speaking tribe of South Africa.

[98] Hottentot. Member of a southern African Negroid people which formerly occupied the region near the Cape. The name comes from the Afrikaans language for "stammered," and which refers to the Hottentots peculiar mode of pronunciation.

[99] Connaught. The westernmost of Ireland's four Provinces. It is made up of the counties of Leitrim, Sligo, Mayo, Roscommon, and Galway.

[100] Theobald Wolfe Tone (1763–1798). Protestant barrister who studied at Trinity College. His *An Argument on behalf of the Catholics of Ireland*, published in 1791, attracted much attention for its insistence that Catholics and Protestants shared much political common ground. In 1796, he negotiated successfully with the French Revolution's Directory for help in leading a rising

in Ireland. Arriving with a French force in September 1798, he was captured and imprisoned. He committed suicide whilst under sentence of death.

[101] Marconi Case. An intricate case of Ministerial knowledge of Government intentions, contracts and share dealing by prominent public figures. The affair centred around the Government's intention to build a chain of state-owned wireless stations, the decision to award the contract for the work to the Marconi Wireless Telegraph Company, and the purchase and sale – for large profits – of Marconi shares by government officials who were in a position to know the effects that the awarding of the Marconi contract would have on its share price. The scandal erupted in 1912 and ran, violently, for some 18 months; it came to light principally as a result of Hilaire Belloc's reporting in his newspaper, the *Eye Witness*. Frances Donaldson in her comprehensive book, *The Marconi Scandal*, published in 1962, says: "It is difficult to present the facts with clarity and justice because of the mass of material among which one is forced to discriminate." Nevertheless, G.K. Chesterton, 23 years after the close of the case, wrote: "It is the fashion to divide recent history into Pre-War and Post-War conditions. I believe it is almost as essential to divide them into the Pre-Marconi and Post-Marconi days."

[102] *Falsus in uno, falsus in omnibus.* In English, "false in one thing, false in all things."

[103] John Redmond (1856–1918). Born of Catholic landed gentry, Redmond became an MP for the Nationalist Irish Parliamentary Party in 1881. Following the party split and bitter strife caused by the Parnell crisis (*vide supra*), Redmond became head of the re-united Nationalist Party and led it from 1900 to 1918. Committed exclusively to Parliamentary agitation, he became alienated from the real feelings of the Irish in the pre- and post-1916 Rising period. He supported Irish enlistment in the British Army during WWI believing that this would provide Irish unity after the war and validate the right of "small nations" to their independence. Unhappily, he failed in all that he sought to achieve.

[104] Eamon De Valera (1882–1975). Irish republican leader who inspired, and still inspires, both intense devotion and intense hatred amongst the Irish. Served as President of the Dáil (the Irish Parliament) from 1919 to 1922. Having rejected the 1922 Treaty which Michael Collins negotiated in the main for the setting up of the Irish Free State (and thereupon resigning his presidency), he took part in the disastrous Civil War (1922–1923) which led to the defeat of the anti-Treaty forces. In later years, he became President of the Irish Republic (1937), turning now against the extra-parliamentary IRA, now against the Blue Shirts of Eoin O'Duffy. A commit-

ted Parliamentarian, "Dev" is still regarded as an enigma.

[105] A reference to Thomas Carlyle's remark upon the death of Louis XV of France (1710-1774), from Chapter 3 of "The Diamond Necklace," published in *Critical and Miscellaneous Essays*, which cover the period from 1830 to 1875.

[106] *Salle des pas perdus.* "The hall of wasted footsteps." A phrase used to refer to the large antechambers leading into important government courts or offices.

[107] Sir Arthur Conan Doyle (1859–1930). Best known for his creation of the detective Sherlock Holmes, the personification of sharp reasoning. The character made Doyle, by 1920, one of the most highly paid writers in the world, though he had started out in 1885 as a qualified eye specialist. His first Holmes story, *A Study in Scarlet*, appeared in 1887. Though educated by Jesuits, he lost the Faith and became interested in the occult; in 1925 he opened the Psychic Bookshop in London. He recorded his psychic experiences in *The Edge of the Unknown* (1930).

[108] Sir William Crookes (1832–1919). A leading Victorian scientist, he made many contributions to the development of Physics and Chemistry. He is best remembered for the Crookes Vacuum Tube, which led to the discovery of X Rays and the electron. Also a famous Spiritualist.

[109] Charing Cross. One of the main central London railway stations which is a stone's throw from Trafalgar Square.

[110] *Nash's Magazine.* London monthly fiction magazine which was in print under various names from 1909 to 1937; merged with *The Pall Mall Magazine* in 1914, becoming *Nash's Pall Mall Magazine.*

[111] Edward D. Morel. English humanitarian and journalist. Having worked in the Belgian Congo, he saw the abuses consequent on Imperialism. In 1903, he published the book, *The Black Man's Burden*. His work brought him into contact with Roger Casement.

[112] "The Pious Editor's Creed," Letter Six from *The Biglow Papers* (1848) by American poet James Russell Lowell (1819-1891).

[113] A reference to the case of the Norwegian, Adolf Beck, living in London, who was sent to prison in 1896 for allegedly perpetrating fraud against women. He was, however, a victim of mistaken identity; the crimes were committed by a "John Smith." Beck had been a petty criminal, but the case records show that his conviction was scandalous in the extreme.

[114] Oscar Slater was a German Jew, real name Leschzinger, who was sentenced to death in 1909 for the murder of Marion Gilchrist in Glasgow, Scotland. The case seemed flimsy to some, and attracted Conan Doyle's

attention. After three years of investigation, Doyle published *The Case of Oscar Slater* (1912). Over the course of the next 15 years, various facts came to light that caused the commutation of Slater's sentence in 1927. Slater spent 18 years in prison and was never compensated for the error.

[115] Putumayo. A region of Columbia and Peru near the river of the same name, where ca. 30,000 natives died as a result of crop exploitation and horrendous conditions of forced labor imposed by the leaders of the Anglo-Peruvian rubber industry for the harvesting of rubber during the late 19th and early 20th century. The "Putumayo Affair" was documented for the British government by Sir Roger Casement (*vide supra*).

[116] Charles Peace (1832–1879). One of the great personalities of the English criminal class of the nineteenth century. Crippled in a steel mill accident in 1846, he began a career of crime. Beginning with theft, he moved on to burglary. He was often caught and imprisoned. However, he eventually ended up killing a policeman on one job and killing the husband of an alleged lover on another. He was hanged for the latter crime.

[117] A reference to the case of serial murders carried out in the East End of London, England, in the 1880's, in which 5 women were murdered. Although the case is still "officially" a mystery, it is now largely agreed that the murderer was a physician with high-level contacts in the Establishment. Most people believe that the killer was Dr. William Gull, the Royal Physician and Freemason, who was covering up Prince Albert's involvement with one of the murdered prostitutes.

[118] *Westminster Gazette*. London daily paper launched in 1839; merged with the *Daily News* in 1928, which became the *News Chronicle* in 1930 when it was absorbed by the *Daily Chronicle*, and ceased publication in 1960.

[119] Reginald John Campbell (1867–1956). A liberal Anglican cleric, whose "universalism" tended to produce a dogma-less "Christianity" – so much so that Alice Bailey, the occultist founder of the New Age movement, could quote him positively. He was the Canon of Chichester Cathedral, England from 1930 to 1946. Chesterton frequently attacked Campbell's liberalism in books and articles.

[120] A reference to the Battle of the River Boyne which took place on July 1, 1690, between James II and William, Prince of Orange. The Boyne battle took place some four miles west of Drogheda, Ireland. The battle itself was inconclusive, but shortly afterwards James II sailed to France and exile, thus consummating the "Glorious Revolution" and ensuring the Protestant and Plutocratic domination of England (*vide supra*).

[121] A passage from Kettle's response to attempts by Rudyard Kipling to fan

Irish Impressions 143

the flames of civil war in Ireland, presumably in line with Carson's efforts to ensure the Home Rule would not apply to the North. Quoted by his wife, Mary Sheehy Kettle, in the memoir she contributed to his *The Ways of War* (1917). The lines run as follows:

> The poet, for a coin,
> Hands to the gabbling rout
> A bucketful of Boyne
> To put the sunrise out.

[122] The Irish National Land League. Founded in Dublin in October, 1879, by Michael Davitt, it was the key organization in the main phase of the 1879–1882 "Land War," which sought to eliminate the landlordism which was then prevalent. Charles Parnell (*vide supra*) became its President, leading to its rapid extension throughout the country. The Land Act of 1881 undermined the unity of the League, because it divided those who merely wanted some reform from those who wanted wholesale, revolutionary change; the League was banned by the British government in October, 1881.

[123] Hubert George De Burgh-Canning (1832-1916), 15th Earl of Clanricarde. The Burke family – or "de Burgh" prior to the name's anglicization – descends from the Norman de Burgh line, the first member of which came to Ireland in the 12th century. Ulick de Burgh received the title Earl of Clanricarde from Henry VIII of England in exchange for his cooperation with Henry's "Surrender and Regrant" scheme, which saw Irish nobles ceding their land to Henry, only to receive it back, with a legal guarantee, if they recognized both Henry's sovereignty over Ireland and his title "Head of the Church." De Burgh was one of the first nobles to cooperate with Henry's plan, in exchange for which he received 6 baronies of land in Galway County. Hubert George became notorious as a landlord in the 19th century as a result of his refusal to grant tolerable terms to the peasant tenants of his estate, which he inherited in 1874 and consisted of 56,826 acres of County Galway. During the agricultural crisis of the winters of 1878-1879, he refused to lower his tenants' rents, and forcibly evicted those that couldn't pay. Many evictions resulted in bloodshed and prison sentences for the tenants; one lasted several days and became known as the "Siege of Saunder's Fort." By 1891 roughly 200 families had been evicted from his estate. Clanricarde was rarely out of the headlines, and he earned for himself the nickname "Lord Clanrackrent."

[124] Clan-na-Gael. The oldest Irish Republican group in the world seeking a 32-County United Ireland, founded sometime between 1867 and 1870 in America; secretly known as the United Brotherhood.

[125] Arthur Balfour (1848–1930). Elected to Parliament in 1874, he became leader of the House of Commons in 1892, and Prime Minister in 1902. Most famous for the Balfour Declaration which declared for a Jewish National Homeland in Palestine. Though opposed to Home Rule, he supported measures to alleviate the non-owning condition of the Irish peasantry, such as Wyndham's Land Purchase Act of 1903.

[126] The Limerick Treaty. Signed on October 3, 1691, it brought to an end the Williamite War, which, following James II's flight to France, had shifted to Ireland, where James landed in 1690 along with French troops in hopes of regaining his throne and restoring Ireland to the Irish. Though James fled back to France after his defeat at the Battle of the Boyne (*vide supra*), the Catholic French and Irish forces continued to fight until forced to cease hostilities at Limerick. The Treaty stipulated that in return for the surrender of their last stronghold in Limerick, the Jacobite soldiers would be granted free passage to France where they would be incorporated into the French army under Louis XIV as the "Irish Brigade," and the Irish would be free to practice their Catholic religion. The English honoured the terms of the treaty by imposing the repressive Penal Laws.

[127] *Kathleen-na-Hulahan*. A reference to the poem of James Mangan (*vide supra*).

[128] Donnybrook Fair. In 1204 King John of England granted a licence to Dublin Corporation to hold an annual 8 day Fair in the village of Donnybrook. It became very popular down the centuries, becoming longer in the process, and becoming, too, a by-word for disorder and drunkenness; though the worst problem was actually noise. The Fair was finally suppressed by the authorities in 1855.

[129] From "Into the Twilight," by W.B. Yeats (1865–1939), published in *The Wind Among the Reeds* (1899).

[130] A reference to the epic poem written by one of England's greatest poets, John Milton (1608–1674).

[131] A reference to the epic poem, *The Rime of the Ancient Mariner*, written by Samuel Taylor Coleridge (1772–1834).

[132] Eft. A newt.

[133] Charles Rowley (1839–?). Socialist who worked in the Ancoats district of Manchester from 1872 to bring cultural recreation to the poor and working class, in the form of artistic and cultural displays, concerts, and adult education. Rowley was connected with the founding of the Ancoats Art Museum (1877), the Ancoats Recreation Committee (1882), and the University Settlement of the University of Manchester (1895).

Irish Impressions 145

[134] *Verecundia.* Latin for "shame."

[135] Probably a reference to the Ulster Unionist Convention of 1892 in Belfast, organized as an attempt to show that the movement for Irish Union was broad-based and popular. It declared unabashedly that it saw Home Rule as an attempt to destroy Protestantism in Ireland, and resolved to support Unionists everywhere. Follow-on rallies took place notably in 1912; Bonar Law (*vide infra*) was present to pledge the support of the English Conservative (and Liberal Unionist) party for the Unionist cause.

[136] Orange Brotherhood. A Protestant political society dedicated to sustaining the "glorious and immortal" memory of King William III and his victory at the Battle of the Boyne. It was instituted in September 1795 in the inn owned by James Sloan in the village of Loughgall, in Ulster, following the victory of the Orange Boys over the "Defenders" at the Battle of the Diamond, one of the last of the continuing battles between Protestant supporters of William of Orange and Catholic supporters of James II. In modern times, it is an important adjunct to Ulster Unionism, with most leaders of the latter in the twentieth century coming from the ranks of Orangeism.

[137] Cobden Club. Established in 1866 to perpetuate the ideas of Richard Cobden (*vide infra*).

[138] Richard Cobden (1804–1865). English reformer and Free Trade capitalist, whose successful crusade to repeal the protectionist Corn Laws made a lasting name for him as an advocate of liberal, unrestricted trade and commerce as the key to national and international prosperity, a position which had a close affinity to that advocated by continental liberal Frédéric Bastiat. The industrialists and merchants of the major cities of England and the North of Ireland fully supported Cobden's demand for repeal of protectionist laws which tended to favor aristocratic landowners to the detriment of the merchant class. Cobden's movement was the foundation of the Manchester School of economic liberalism.

[139] Joseph Chamberlain (1836–1914). A successful businessman and MP from Birmingham, elected in 1876 as a Liberal. He resigned from the Liberal government in 1886 over its support for Irish Home Rule (which he opposed), and led those who followed him – the Liberal *Unionists* – in an alliance with the Conservative Party to oppose it. By the turn of the century he became the premier advocate of Tariff Reform – protectionist laws designed to form the British Empire into a single trading bloc.

[140] Andrew Bonar Law (1858–1923). Ulster Presbyterian, he became leader of the Conservative Party in 1911, and was British Prime Minister from October 1922 to May 1923. His political hero and inspiration in

Tariff Reform was Joseph Chamberlain (*vide supra*). Unreservedly opposed to Irish independence or even Home Rule, he declared at Blenheim Palace on June 29, 1912, that there was "no length of resistance to which Ulster can go in which I would not be prepared to support them."

[141] Probably a reference to George Clark, Sr. (1843–1901), Freemason, Unionist, and head of the marine engineering firm Messrs Geo. Clark, Ltd.; or to his son, George Clark, Jr. (1865–1937). May alternatively be a reference to Sir George Clark (1861–1935) of Belfast, leading shipbuilder and Unionist.

[142] Rudyard Kipling (1865–1936). English short story writer, novelist and poet. He celebrated the alleged achievements of British Imperialism, gaining much popularity with his poem, *The White Man's Burden* (1899). His most famous works are: *The Jungle Book* (1894), *The Man Who Would Be King* (1888/9), *The Seven Seas* (1896), and his probable masterpiece, *Kim* (1901). He was the first Englishman to win the Nobel Prize for Literature, which he was awarded in 1907.

[143] St. John Irvine (1883–1971). A playwright, novelist and Unionist. He started out with the Fabian Society and progressed to writing for A. R. Orage's *New Age*. He met W.B. Yeats and came to support Irish Home Rule, flamboyantly detesting Edward Carson. He looked to Horace Plunkett and George Russell for a New Ireland, but he came to have "a pathological hatred of the rest of Ireland" after the 1916 Rebellion and the subsequent War of Independence.

[144] Molly Algood (1887–1952). Actress who performed under the stage name Máire O'Neill. Well known on stage, she appeared in over 40 films in a long career. Married the actor Arthur Sinclair, who appeared in over a dozen films himself.

[145] A reference to the Royal Mail Ship *Leinster*, which was sunk off the Dublin coast on October 10, 1918, by three torpedoes launched from the German U-Boat 123. Some 500 people lost their lives as a result.

[146] Puck to Pickwick. Characters from novels written by Charles Dickens (1812–1870).

ST. PATRICK'S CATHEDRAL, DUBLIN.

> "The Irish Question is at bottom a war against Protestantism; it is an attempt to establish a Roman Catholic ascendancy in Ireland to begin the disintegration of the Empire by securing a second parliament in Dublin."
>
> —Dr. William McKean, Irish Presbyterian Church
> Ulster Hall, September 28, 1912

Further Reading

For those interested in a deeper study of Ireland and its long and complex history, the following selection of works is provided, with emphasis in particular on the modern period and the struggle for Independence. The Directors do not necessarily endorse every aspect of these works; they are offered, however, as points of departure for a study of the issues.

How the Irish Saved Civilization, by Thomas Cahill (London: Hodder & Stoughton, 1995). A broad survey of Irish history from the fall of Rome to the rise of Medieval Europe, which provides many fascinating details.

The Easter Rebellion, by Max Caulfield (Dublin: Gill & MacMillan, 1995). Deals only with the actual Rebellion itself, but in remarkable detail.

Tans, Terror and the Troubles, by T. Ryle Dwyer. (Cork: Mercier Press, 2001). A history of the Irish Republican struggle in Kerry from 1913–1923 as a microcosm of what happened throughout Ireland in the period leading up to and including the War of Independence.

Michael Collins: A Life, by James Mackay (Edinburgh: Mainstream Publishing, 1997). One of the best biographies of Michael Collins available.

Big Fellow, Long Fellow: A Joint Biography of Collins and De Valera, by T. Ryle Dwyer (Dublin: Gill & MacMillan, 1998). A unique double biography that looks at the two main actors in the Irish struggle in the twentieth century, and how they related, positively and negatively, to one another.

Michael Collins: In His Own Words, edited by Francis Costello (Dublin: Gill & MacMillan, 1997). An interesting selection of Collins's writings with sympathetic commentary that places the writings in their historical and political context.

Michael Collins and the Brotherhood, by Vincent MacDowell (Dublin: Ashfield Press, 1997). Probably the definitive work on the question of who was responsible for the "mysterious" murder of

Collins. Demonstrates that the idea that Anti-Treaty IRA forces were responsible is not tenable.

Brother Against Brother, by Liam Deasy (Cork: Mercier Press, 1998). A moving work by the former chief of the celebrated Cork Brigade of the IRA, who joined the Anti-Treaty forces during the Irish Civil War. Brings out the full anguish and passion of the period, but in a sympathetic manner that seeks justice for both sides to the conflict.

The IRA and its Enemies: Violence and Community in Cork, 1916–1923, by Peter Hart (Oxford: Clarendon Press, 1998). A well written and well documented history of the IRA in Cork – the most republican of the Irish Counties – which recreates the atmosphere of fear and loyalty during the War of Independence.

Harry Boland: A Biography, by Jim Maher (Cork: Mercier Press, 1998). Michael Collins's right hand man, who played a vital, if still unseen, role in the War of Independence. This is the only biography yet published about Boland.

The Irish Counter-Revolution: 1921–1936, by John Regan (Dublin: Gill & MacMillan, 1999). An in-depth study of the Ireland that came out of the Civil War, which looks at how those who claimed to support the Treaty brought back from London by Collins went off in a variety of directions as the years passed: some sought the return of the British Monarchy in one form or another, some looked to the Italian Corporate State, while still others stumbled from one principle and policy to another.

The Tragedy of James Connolly, by Fr. Denis Fahey (Hawthorne, CA: OMNI/Christian Books, 1988). A interesting tangent on James Connolly in the form of a lengthy review of a book on Connolly by R.M. Fox, *James Connolly: The Forerunner* (1946).

The Framework of a Christian State, by Fr. E. Cahill, Appendices (Fort Collins, CO: Roman Catholic Books, n.d.). The appendices deal with Irish history generally and the history and state of the Social Question in Ireland during the first part of the 20th century.

About IHS Press

IHS Press believes that the key to the restoration of Catholic Society is the recovery and the implementation of the wisdom our Fathers in the Faith possessed so fully less than a century ago. At a time when numerous ideologies were competing for supremacy, these men articulated, with precision and vigor, and *without* apology or compromise, the only genuine alternative to the then- (and still-) prevailing currents of thought: value-free and yet bureaucratic "progressivism" on the one hand, and the rehashed, *laissez-faire* free-for-all of "conservatism" on the other. That alternative is the Social Teaching of the Catholic Church.

Catholic Social Teaching offers the solutions to the political, economic, and social problems that plague modern society; problems that stem from the false principles of the Reformation, Renaissance, and Revolution, and which are exacerbated by the industrialization and the secularization of society that has continued for several centuries. Defending, explaining, and applying this Teaching was the business of the great Social Catholics of last century. Unfortunately, much of their work is today both unknown and unavailable.

Thus, IHS Press was founded in September of 2001A.D. as the only publisher dedicated exclusively to the Social Teaching of the Church, helping Catholics of the third millennium pick up where those of last century left off. IHS Press is committed to recovering, and *helping others to rediscover,* the valuable works of the Catholic economists, historians, and social critics. To that end, IHS Press is in the business of issuing critical editions of works on society, politics, and economics by writers, thinkers, and men of action such as Hilaire Belloc, Gilbert Chesterton, Arthur Penty, Fr. Vincent McNabb, Fr. Denis Fahey, Jean Ousset, Amintore Fanfani, George O'Brien, and others, making the wisdom they contain available to the current generation.

It is the aim of IHS Press to issue these vitally important works in high-quality volumes and at reasonable prices, to enable the widest possible audience to acquire, enjoy, and benefit from them. Such an undertaking cannot be maintained without the support of generous benefactors. With that in mind, IHS Press was constituted as a not-for-profit corporation which is exempt from federal tax according to Section 501(c)(3) of the United States Internal Revenue Code. Donations to IHS Press are, therefore, tax deductible, and are especially welcome to support its continued operation, and to help it with the publication of new titles and the more widespread dissemination of those already in print.

For more information, contact us at:
222 W. 21st St., Suite F-122-Norfolk, VA 23517-(757) 423-0324
info@ihspress.com   www.ihspress.com   fax: (419) 715-0361

IHS Press is a tax-exempt 501(c)(3) corporation; EIN: 54-2057581.
Applicable documentation is available upon request.

MORE ON CATHOLIC SOCIAL DOCTRINE...

The Free Press
Hilaire Belloc
$8.95 96 pages
paperback
0-9714894-1-6

Belloc's unabashed look at what in his day was the press and in ours is the media. It is the only work of its kind: a critique and analysis of the media from the coherent perspective of a Catholic and a Distributist.

Belloc makes the connection between capitalism, finance, and the press, while explaining the theoretical and practical evils besetting the modern media as a creature of our economic and political system. The essay is both a criticism of media manipulation, control, and suppression of news and opinion in support of the liberal order of capitalism and so-called democracy, and a call for a Free Press – one free to report accurate news and sponsor an intelligent and serious exchange of ideas. Included is a new Preface which looks thoroughly at the modern media and discusses what makes Belloc's writing so relevant today.

The Outline of Sanity
G.K. Chesterton
$14.95 183 pages
paperback
0-9714894-0-8

Chesterton wrote *The Outline* as a lively and commonsense – yet rigorous – examination of how both Capitalism and Socialism work in the real world. He looked at their effect on families, homes, and men. He did "economics" as if it still had something to do with households.

The Outline is not just a stinging critique of modern economic life by an intelligent, brutally honest writer. It is an introduction to an alternative perspective, one that transcends old dichotomies and offers a vision of an economic order which, rather than dominating man, actually serves him.

Action
Jean Ousset
$16.95 272 pages
paperback
0-9714894-2-4

A manual for today's Catholic Crusader by one of the late 20th century's most respected and knowledgeable Catholic laymen.

Ousset, a foremost scholar of the Revolution, and a leader of the European anti-Marxist movement, founded *La Cité Catholique* in France in 1946 to spread the Social Reign of Christ. *Action* is one of his thorough, engaging, and practical manuals designed to inspire, motivate, and guide the modern Catholic layman in the understanding and performance of his duty to fight, with every available and lawful means, for the implementation of Catholic principles in society.

Includes a short Preface by Mr. Anthony Fraser, and a comprehensive introduction by the Publisher.

AVAILABLE AT FINE BOOKSTORES...

AVAILABLE FROM IHS PRESS.

The Restoration of Property
Hilaire Belloc
$8.95 96 pages
paperback
0-9714894-4-0

The famous Distributist tract: a clear, concise sketch of how a society of real property owners might be re-established and defended.

Re-established: civilized society up until the last 150 years consisted largely of independent owners of real property. Though such a situation is incomprehensible today, it was not so long ago that men possessed real freedom to control their own destiny. Belloc's outline is just one of many possible glimpses of what such a situation might look like.

Defended: once established, such a society must be maintained by consensus, custom, and law. Absent these, economic life is all too productive of scandals reminiscent of Enron, WorldCom, and countless others. Just as some in the not-too-distant past choose to inaugurate social-Darwinist economics, so too may men today decide to move society in a different direction. All it takes is a vision, and a sense of how to implement that vision; Belloc's *Essay* provides both.

Utopia of Usurers
G.K. Chesterton
$11.95 136 pages
paperback
0-9714894-3-2

This is Chesterton at his energetic and boisterous best, taking on the economic and cultural apostles of capitalism. *Utopia* is a collection of articles written in 1913–1915 for the *Daily Herald*. What results is a full-scale broadside against the folly of modern economic and cultural life, in the name of justice and charity.

With classic wit and rigorous logic, GKC points out how all aspects of life have suffered tremendously from an attitude that makes financial and material gain the End of life, at the expense of those higher and human values without which life is hardly worth living.

This new edition of *Utopia* features a Preface by Mr. Aidan Mackey, English Chesterton scholar of singular renown. Born in Manchester, England, in 1922, Mackey founded the Distributist Association in 1947, and soon after became editor of *The Distributist*, which saw publication from 1953–1960. Mackey wrote *Mr. Chesterton Comes to Tea* (1979); *The Wisdom of GKC* (1986), currently being re-edited in a new edition for the Catholic Truth Society of England; and *Hilaire Belloc and His Critics* (1991).

Order direct today: by phone, fax, mail, e-mail, online.
s/h: $3.00 per book; $1.00 ea. add'l. book. Check, m.o., VISA, MC.

222 W. 21ˢᵗ St., Suite F–122~Norfolk, VA 23517~(757) 423–0324
order@ihspress.com www.ihspress.com fax: (419) 715-0361

OR ORDER DIRECT FROM IHS PRESS.